Symbolist Art in Poland

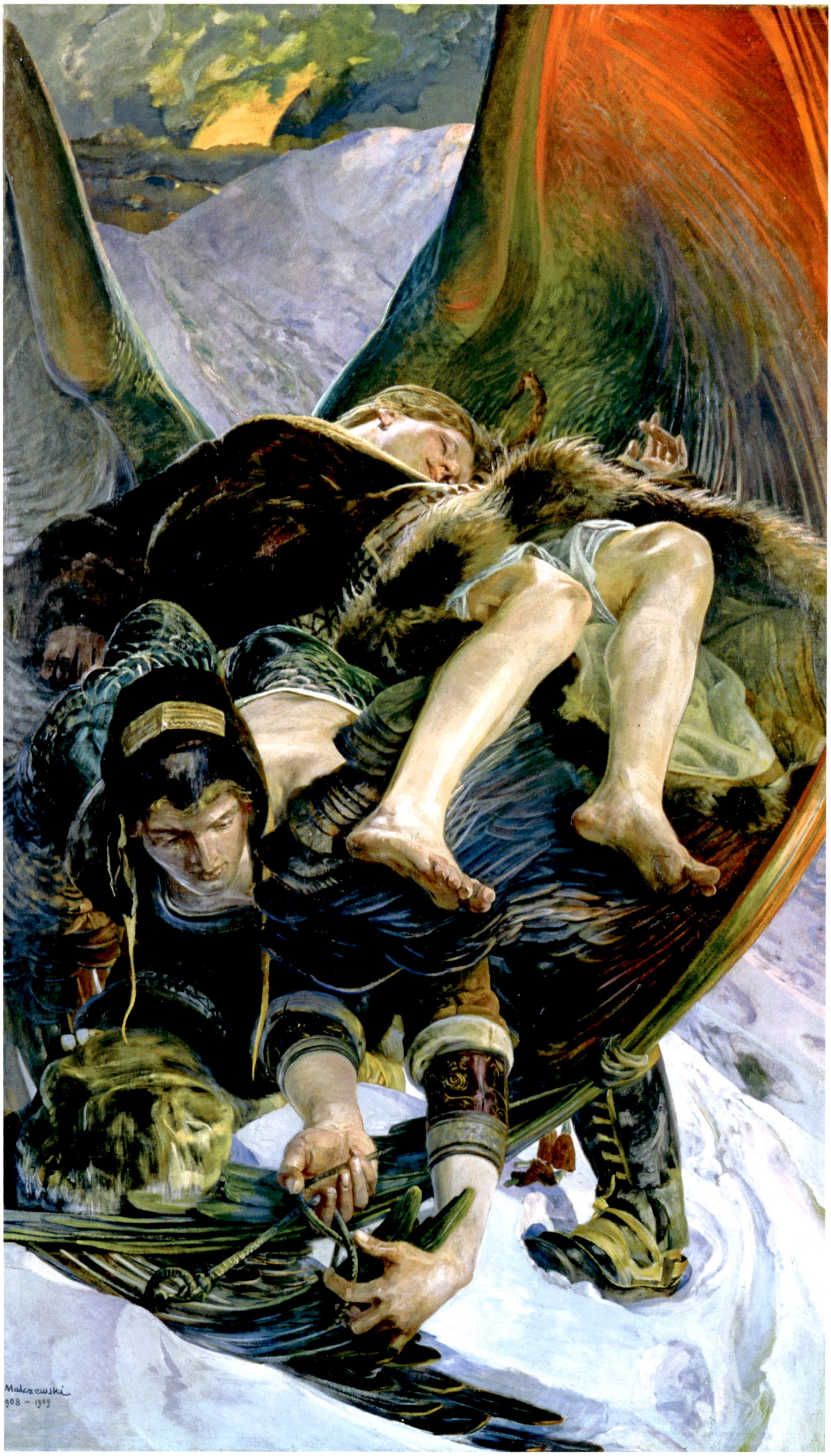
Malczewski
908 – 1909

Symbolist Art in Poland

Poland and Britain c.1900

Edited by Alison Smith

TATE PUBLISHING

First published 2009 by order of the Tate Trustees
by Tate Publishing, a division of Tate Enterprises Ltd,
Millbank, London SW1P 4RG
www.tate.org.uk/publishing

on the occasion of the exhibition
Symbolist Art in Poland
Tate Britain, London
14 March – 21 June 2009

British Library Cataloguing in Publication Data
A catalogue record for this book is available from the British Library

ISBN 978 1 85437 853 8

Designed by Susan Wightman at Libanus Press
Printed by CS Graphics

Publication coincides with the *Polish Culture Series in the UK 2009–2010* which is organised by the Adam Mickiewicz Institute.

Front cover: Kazimierz Sichulski, *Angel* 1911 (detail of fig.25)
Frontispiece: Jacek Malczewski, *Eloe with Ellenai* 1908–9 (detail of fig.17)

Measurements of artworks are given in centimetres, height before width.

Contents

Director's Foreword

This display and the accompanying publication further Tate Britain's mission to encourage a broader understanding of the international reach of Tate's historic collection. The connections between British and French art around 1900 have been the focus of a number of Tate exhibitions in recent years, so now seems a timely moment to extend the scope of the dialogue between Britain and the continent to encompass Central Europe. Polish art is not well known in this country largely because of the Second World War and the Iron Curtain. Even less known is the cultural dialogue that existed between the two nations during the period of partition, the focus of this study. With Poland now an active member of the EU, it is not only its art that is ripe for rediscovery but also the historic connections between Poland and Britain that were obscured for much of the twentieth century.

This project was initiated by the Adam Mickiewicz Institute in Warsaw, organiser of the Polish Culture Series in the UK 2009–2010. We are extremely grateful to the Institute for funding both the transportation of loans from Poland to Tate Britain and this publication. I would particularly like to thank Aneta Prasał-Wiśniewska, project co-ordinator at the AMI, for her help in taking the project forward together with Piotr Kopszak, curator at the National Museum in Warsaw, and Andrzej Szczerski, lecturer at the Institute of Art History at the Jagiellonian University in Kraków. They have all worked closely with Tate curator Alison Smith in realising both the display and this book. Thanks also to Jeremy Musson for his help in editing the essay on pages 20–33, and to Julia Dudkiewicz, Collections Manager at the Society of Antiquaries, London, for her diligence in assisting with research for the publication.

STEPHEN DEUCHAR
Director, Tate Britain

British Symbolism and Polish Modernism c.1900

ALISON SMITH

This project was inspired by the exhibition *In the Footsteps of the Pre-Raphaelites*, held in Warsaw in 2006 with the aim of drawing attention to the awareness of progressive British art shown by Polish modernists around the turn of the last century.[1] Given the recent surge of interest in Pre-Raphaelitism both within Britain and abroad, now is an exciting moment to build on the example of this exhibition to encourage a broader, more international understanding of the movement and its offshoots and, in particular, to look beyond the Franco-centric models of modern art which for much of the twentieth century relegated the Pre-Raphaelites to the status of an eccentric, isolationist movement that failed to contribute in any enduring way to the universal formalist language of modernism. As Andrzej Szczerski has recently argued, the adoption of a more dynamic art-historical perspective on Europe that focuses on peripheral areas as well as acknowledged centres like Paris, allows for a more nuanced understanding of the impact British art and design had in Central Europe at this time.[2] From a Polish perspective, British art of that period was modern and progressive, and a lodestar for modernism in Poland in that it was perceived simultaneously as both nationalistic and cosmopolitan. The later phase of the Pre-Raphaelite movement was particularly influential because it enhanced a strong Symbolist strand in Polish visual culture, and was seen to incarnate the concept of *życie* (life) so fundamental to the art produced around 1890–1918. This is the era known as the inaugural period of Polish modernism which came to a close with the declaration of Polish independence at the end of the First World War.

The fact that British art had a greater impact in Poland than vice versa can partly be explained by the cultural policies of the three partitioning powers – Russia, Prussia and Austria – which, as Jan Cavanaugh has explained, operated to prevent international recognition of Polish art as a category.[3] Although the Polish Question was contested on and off in the British press, sympathy for the cause of independence was most marked when Britain was at conflict with one of the occupying powers, as was the case with Russia in the Crimean War of 1853–6, and later with Germany and Austria-Hungary in the First World War. During the early twentieth century, the Anglophone novelist Joseph Conrad (Józef Teodor Konrad Korzeniowski) did much to propagate the cause of independence in his writings, presenting Poland as the victim of German and Russian imperialism. Conrad was one of several Poles who came to stand as a symbol of displaced exile, demonstrating that Polish identity was not just the expression of geopolitical struggles, but of individual creative personalities whose art was seen to both encapsulate the soul of the suffering nation while aspiring towards a moral transcendent ideal.

Chief among these was the pianist and composer Ignacy Jan Paderewski (1860–1941), one of the first international musical celebrities, whose flamboyant public persona was enhanced by his well-publicised activities as a Polish patriot. He later became a statesman and was even briefly Prime Minister of Poland in 1919. Paderewski made his London debut in 1890, becoming an overwhelmingly successful performer, his brilliant technique and personality on stage generating a near mystical devotion. On his first sight of the pianist, the painter Edward Burne-Jones reputedly declared that he had seen 'an Archangel with a splendid halo of golden hair treading the London pavements'.[4] For Burne-Jones, Paderewski's shock of red hair and intense gaze epitomised his ideal of male beauty: 'There's a beautiful fellow in London named Paderewski … and I want to have a face like him and look like him, and I can't – there's trouble. He looks like Swinburne looked at 20 that I could cry over past things.' Burne-Jones' famous pencil drawing of Paderewski (fig.1) was produced the following year, sketched

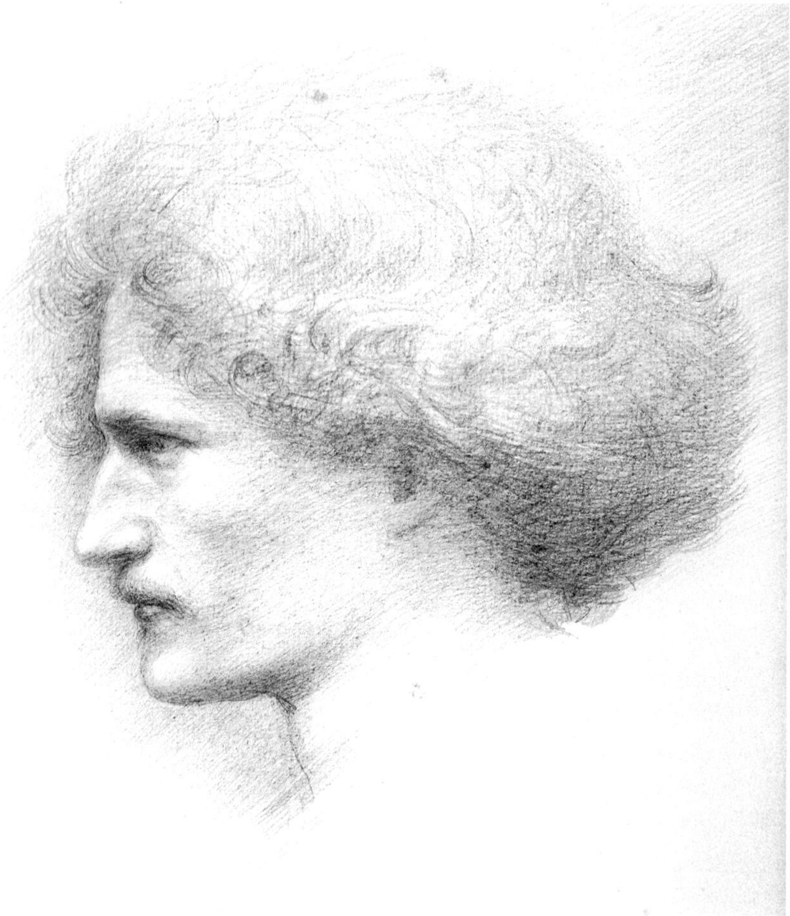

Fig.1 Edward Burne-Jones
Portrait of Ignacy Jan Paderewski
1892
Pencil on paper
34.7 x 31
National Museum Warsaw

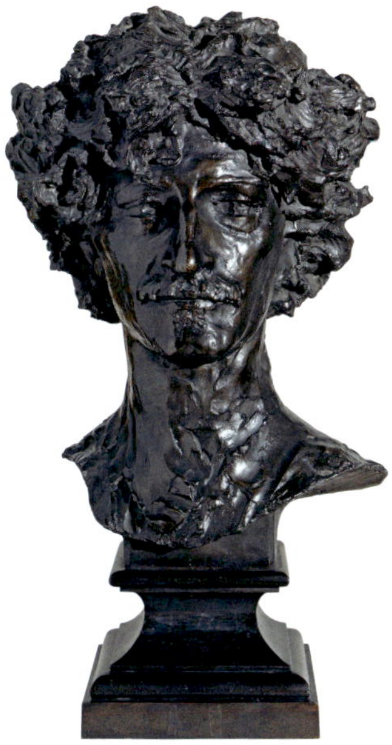

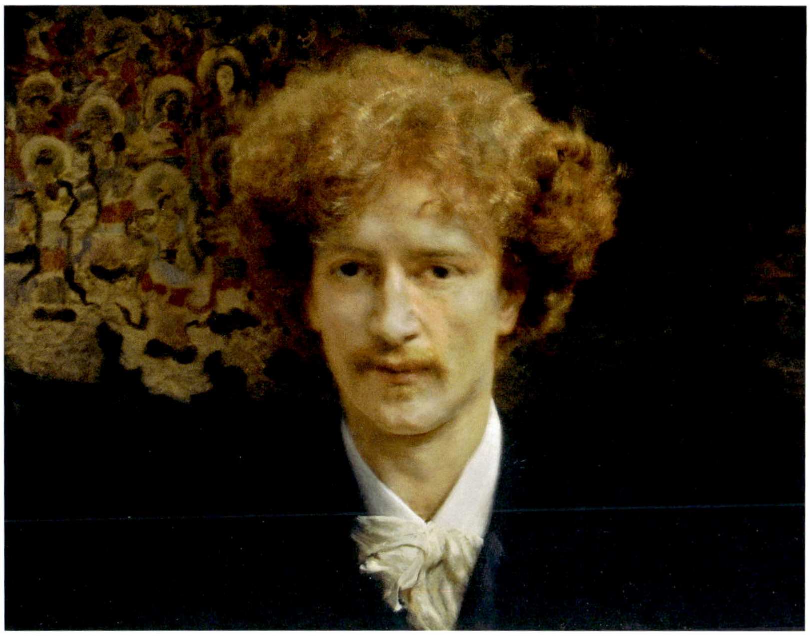

according to the pianist, 'rapidly, even violently', and was presented by the painter to the composer, who later bequeathed it to the National Museum in Warsaw.[5] In his memoir Paderewski erroneously described this work as a silverpoint (the Renaissance technique of draughtsmanship associated with delicate virtuosity), equating the refinement of the artist's technique with the temperament of his own subject. With its sensitive profile, heavily shaded eyes and wispy Botticelli-like hair, this portrait, in the words of T. Martin Wood, represents 'the sympathy between two minds dedicated to beauty … It is a type *spirituel* rather than spiritual, not rejecting life but caring only for the finest it has to offer'.[6] The image was widely disseminated by Paderewski through Frederick Hollyer's photograph of the work, which he regularly gave to selected fans with his autograph or dedication. Paderewski also posed for other British artists, including Alfred Gilbert, who modelled a bust in two hours while the composer played the piano in the sculptor's studio in the summer of 1891 (fig.2). He also performed on several occasions for Lawrence Alma-Tadema at the painter's London residence Townshend House near Regent's Park, and when sitting for the artist (fig.3) also had to contend with Alma-Tadema's wife Laura and the Princess Louise: 'Each one was constantly begging me to turn his way.'[7] Other artists eager to capture Paderewski's motile features included Violet Manners (née Lindsay), one of the avant-garde aesthetes known as the Souls, who produced a delicate drawing published as a lithograph of the composer's face. All these portraits focus on the head of Paderewski, rather than his hands, as both the key to his artistic personality, and as an expression of rarefied beauty.

The 'spirituel' quality that Wood discerned in Burne-Jones' drawing of

Fig.2 Sir Alfred Gilbert
Ignacy Jan Paderewski
1891
Bronze sculpture
60 x 31.9 x 19.3
Tate

Fig.3 Lawrence Alma-Tadema
Portrait of Ignacy Jan Paderewski
1891
Oil on canvas
45.5 x 59
National Museum Warsaw

Paderewski also distinguishes the engravings made after the artist's paintings by Feliks Jasiński, a Pole who later assumed French citizenship. Enraptured by the rare quality of Jasiński's etching after Botticelli's *Primavera*, published by Arthur Tooth in 1892, Burne-Jones alighted upon Jasiński as the perfect engraver to reproduce his works, even going so far as to request that an exception be made to the standard rule of destroying a plate after an edition had been made in the case of Jasiński's plate of his *Annunciation*, which was given to the Victoria and Albert Museum as an example of Jasiński's superlative technique. (The fact that Botticelli practised silverpoint further served to reinforce the link between his art and the aesthetic manner of Jasiński and Burne-Jones.) Between 1894 and 1903 Tooth published six large engravings on vellum after key paintings by Burne-Jones (fig.4), and one sepia etching after Dante Gabriel Rossetti's *Paolo and Francesca* (fig.5). Taking on average a year to produce each plate, Jasiński worked with extreme technical subtlety with the aim of translating the colour of the paintings into monochrome. Highly acclaimed in Europe throughout the 1890s, Jasiński did much to promote Burne-Jones' reputation outside Britain as the greatest Pre-Raphaelite. For Jasiński's biographer, Léopold Wellisz, both artists existed in a similar state of melancholy exile from the world, the affinity between their two temperaments expressed through a shared refinement of line: 'Burne-Jones is not a colourist and in fact his works lose nothing by being reduced to a single colour. Who knows if Jasiński's range of black and white does not render better the charm and the idealised beauty of the symbolism than the original works in colour?'[8]

Fig.4 Feliks Jasiński
The Golden Stairs
1894
Engraving on parchment
75 x 36.5
National Museum Warsaw

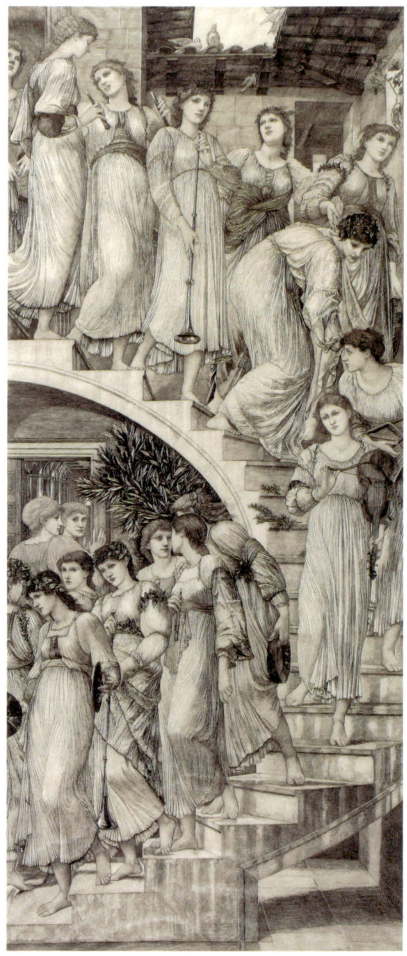

Around the turn of the century, Polish art as a category, rather than the work of isolated individuals, became more widely known in Britain through the *Sztuka* (Art) secessionist society. Based in Kraków, *Sztuka* was the main organ of Polish modernism, embracing indigenous traits as well as cosmopolitan stylistic trends. It was through its inclusion in international exhibitions that *Sztuka* attracted critical attention, as evinced by the articles on the movement by Amelia Sarah Levetus, a British critic based in Vienna, which appeared in *The Studio* in the early years of the twentieth century. Levetus' review of the Polish section of the 1906 London International Exhibition was particularly significant in equating the tragedy of Poland with its progressive art and spirit of nationality, as well as in illuminating the work of some of the most prominent artists within the movement, including Stanisław Wyspiański, Józef Mehoffer (whose *Strange Garden*, see fig.19, was reproduced in the feature) and Jacek Malczewski, describing *The Death of Ellenai* (see fig.16) in powerful emotive terms.[9] Levetus' notion of suffering as a prerequisite for prophetic insight in an artist found an even more trenchant form of expression in the writer Katherine Mansfield's poem *To Stanislaw Wyspianski*, conceived around the time of the artist's death in 1907, although not published until 1938. This extraordinary piece of verse shows how Polish

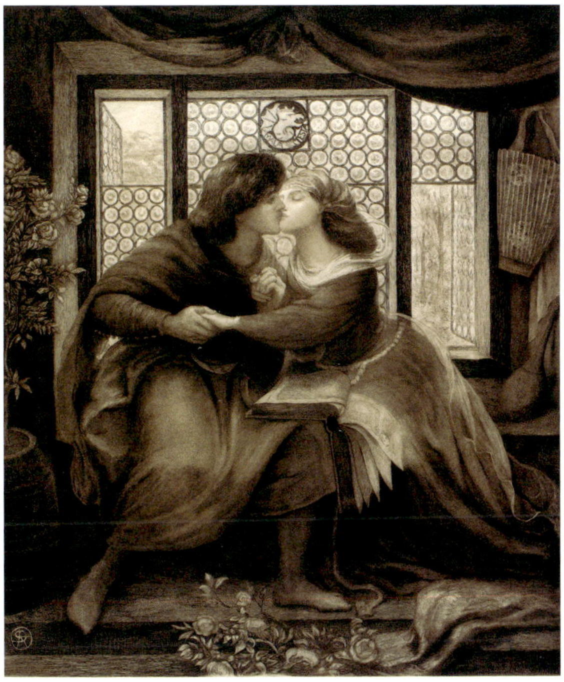

Fig.5 Feliks Jasiński
Paolo and Francesca
1903
Etching in sepia tone on paper
46.8 x 37.9
National Museum Warsaw

culture offered the occasion for an extreme romantic mode, for a society otherwise steeped in Edwardian nostalgia, providing an intense vehicle of expression especially for disenfranchised women dissatisfied with what they perceived as the complacency of contemporary bourgeois society:

> Yours a more personal labour than the Nazarene's miracles,
> Yours a more forceful encounter than the Nazarene's gentle commands.
> Stanislaw Wyspianski – Oh man with the name of a fighter,
> Across these thousands of sea-shattered miles we cry and proclaim you;
> We say 'He is lying in Poland, and Poland thinks
> he is dead;
> But he gave the denial to Death – he is lying there,
> wakeful;
> The blood in his giant heart pulls red through his
> veins.'[10]

Within Poland, as we have already noted, British culture was regarded as dynamic and progressive, the expression of the most advanced industrial nation, and the first to relate mass production to artistic and cultural development. For the late-romantic poet Cyprian Kamil Norwid, the Great Exhibition of 1851 was the fulcrum for design reform and equality in the arts, principles extolled in his poem *Promethidon*, published in Paris that year. Paderewski later recalled that when he arrived in London in 1890, 'life was at its richest and highest then. It was a great flowering of that English civilisation'.[11] Despite the example of British culture for the development of modernity within Poland, there is little evidence of Polish artists visiting Britain, notable exceptions being Józef Pankiewicz, in London between 1897 and 1906, and Anna Bilińska-Bohdanowicz and Teodor Axentowicz, who each visited London in the early 1890s, inspired by the British portraiture tradition. A number of other painters worked in St Petersburg, Berlin and Munich – the latter a centre that attracted British artists during the nineteenth century. Access to British art also came through the large-scale international exhibitions staged in Munich, Berlin, Vienna, Budapest and Paris. The latter was a magnet for Polish artists, being financially and linguistically more accessible than Britain, and it was not only here that many artists trained and worked, but where they were exposed to the works of the British school. Around 1890 at least twelve key Polish modernists were in the city, including Mehoffer (1891–6), Pankiewicz (1889–90), Wyspiański (1891–6), and Olga Boznańska, who settled permanently in Paris from 1889, she and Pankiewicz taking a lead from the Anglo-French art of James Abbott McNeill Whistler. Paris was also significant for being the capital that sparked international interest in the Pre-Raphaelite circle, especially the later Symbolist strain within the movement epitomised by Burne-Jones. His works were exhibited at a number of Parisian venues from 1885 to 1895, the appreciation of his art further encouraged by Jasiński's prints. Enthusiasm for Burne-Jones peaked with the exhibition of *King Cophetua and the Beggar Maid* 1884 (Tate) at the Paris Universal Exhibition of 1889, for which the artist was awarded the Legion of Honour. It was through the mediation of French art criticism that the work of artists such as Burne-Jones, G.F. Watts and Aubrey Beardsley attained a key status within the pan-European Symbolist movement, by virtue of its decorative 'Art Nouveau' qualities and symbolic ambiguity. The French also employed the term 'Pre-Raphaelite' to describe a vague neo-romantic literary aesthetic, which was how the movement was comprehended in Poland.

The perceived national character of British art was especially relevant at the time of Poland's political non-existence, hence the large number of publications in Polish of literary, theoretical and critical texts, often via the translations of French writers. Robert de la Sizeranne's *Ruskin and the Cult of Beauty* (translated by Antoni Potocki 1898), and *Contemporary Painting in England* (translated by Helena d'Abancourt 1901) were very influential, the latter illustrating iconic works such as Watts' *Hope* 1886 (fig.6), Rossetti's *Beata Beatrix c.*1864–70 (both Tate) and Burne-Jones' *The Wheel of Fortune* 1875–83 (Musée d'Orsay). Of further importance were the publications of selected writings by John Ruskin and William Morris, Leon Winiarski's biography of the latter (published in 1900) also being particularly influential. The writings of Walter Pater were known through reviews and the translations that appeared after 1909.[12] Reproductions of works by Burne-Jones, Rossetti and Beardsley appeared in the periodical *Chimera*, edited by Zenon Przesmycki and published in Warsaw between 1901 and 1907, the September 1901 edition including a reproduction of Beardsley's *The Return of Tannhäuser to the Venusberg* 1895 (fig.7).[13] Among its reproductions, the *Tygodnik Ilustrowany* (*Illustrated Weekly*), established in Warsaw in 1859, published Ford Madox Brown's *Cromwell on his Farm* 1873–4 (Lady Lever Art Gallery, Liverpool) on the cover of its 1898 issue. The Kraków journal *Życie*, edited by Stanisław Przybyszewski with Wyspiański as art editor and the main vehicle of the 'Young Poland' ('*Młoda Polska*') modernist movement, made a hero of Burne-Jones, dedicating a special supplement to a reproduction of the silverpoint of Paderewski.[14] Other reproductions could be purchased by collectors from sources such as the Altenberg bookshop in Lvov, and international periodicals like *The Studio* were available through subscription. Actual reviews of works by British artists were rare, the most notable being the essay included by the aesthete and collector of Japanese art Feliks Jasieński in his book *Manggha: Promenades à travers le monde, l'art et les idées*, published in France in 1901. Repudiating the charge made by the writer Max Nordau in his influential book *Degeneration* (first published in Germany in 1893) that Pre-Raphaelitism was a regressive tendency, being merely derivative of Italian Renaissance art, Jasieński extolled the movement for its concern with truth and poetry, and for elevating the artist's vision above painterly technique, objectives that distinguished them from the Impressionists. Discussing the paintings on display at the National Gallery in London, Jasieński alighted on John Everett Millais' *A Yeoman of the Guard* 1876 (Tate),

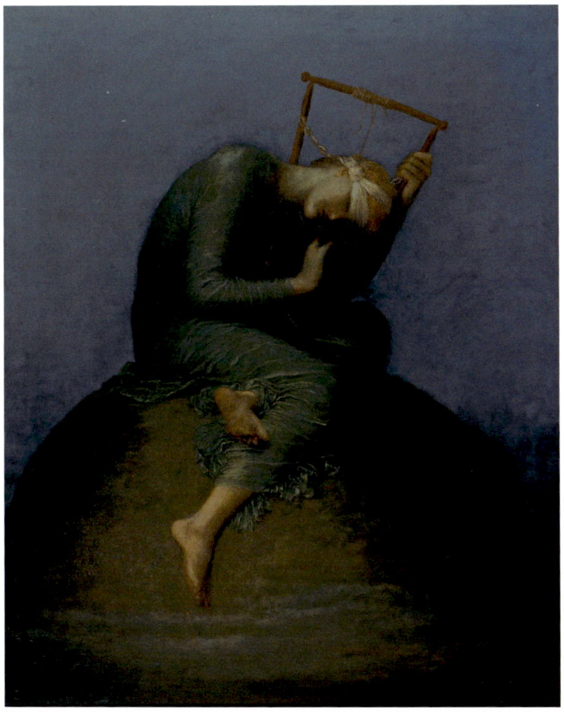

Fig.6 George Frederic Watts
Hope
1886
Oil on canvas
142.2 x 111.8
Tate

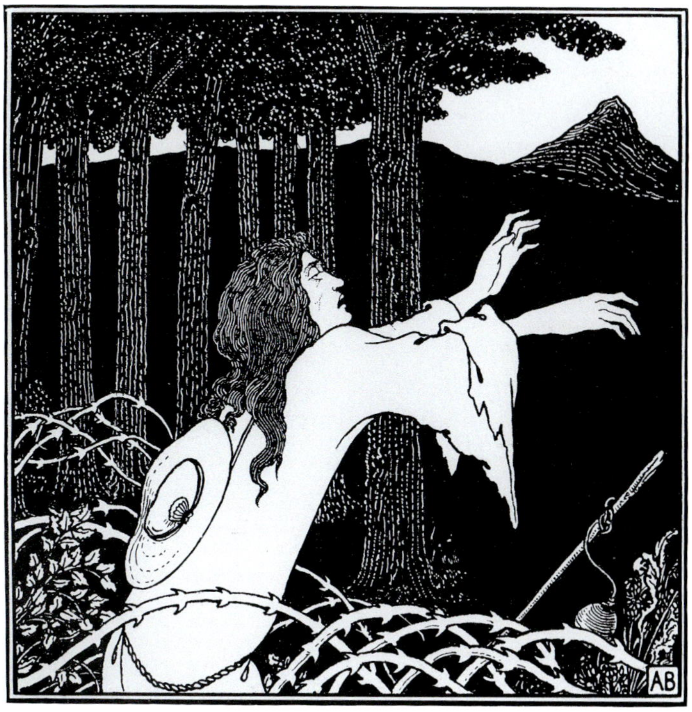

Fig.7 Aubrey Beardsley
The Return of Tannhäuser to the Venusberg, from 'The Story of Venus and Tannhäuser'
1895
Lithograph
Private Collection

describing it as a feast for the eye, an extraordinary symphony of colour. However, he felt that Burne-Jones' *Vespertina Quies* 1893 (Tate), although a formally less accomplished work, communicated a higher ideal, being more expressive of 'the optimistic spirit of the artist's poetic soul'.[15]

The importance accorded to personality, or the idea of the soul of the artist inscribed within a work, is a key example of how Pre-Raphaelite art was 'Polonised' in the cause of promoting Polish identity. Sizeranne's view that Pre-Raphaelite painting was completely separate from any other form of contemporary art, and therefore an English school of national art, gained currency within Poland among factions concerned to advance the notion of Polish independence co-existing with progress within the arts. In the preface to her Polish translation of Sizeranne's *Contemporary Painting in England*, Helena d'Abancourt made the case that the autonomous Pre-Raphaelite school provided the model for a distinct national school within Poland, a view echoed by Jasieński, who saw in Watts a supreme example of self-sacrifice:

> I consider the silent hours that I have spent in the studio-house at Holland Park Road as the greatest in my entire life. The works exhibited there only have the best influence on the soul of the viewer and this was the artist's only concern. He gave a part of his life's work to the country and one can admire it in the museum dedicated to English art. His studio is open to the public not because of his vanity or his need to promote his work which would have been the case in three out of four instances on the continent, but because the works exhibited here contain thought, because the artist teaches and not entertains, because life is serious.[16]

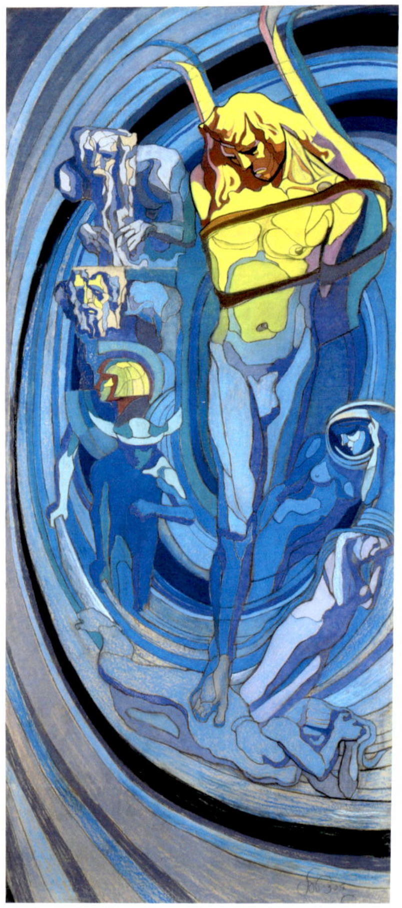

Fig.8 Stanisław Wyspiański
Apollo
1904
Pastel on paper
343 x 146
National Museum Kraków

Although it would be true to say that the art of key figures like Watts and Burne-Jones helped to sustain the messianic trajectory of Polish art, Pre-Raphaelitism was not treated as a direct source of influence. Rather, merging with a range of European traditions, it functioned as a movement with which contemporary Polish artists could identify.The most obvious shared element was the romantic vein in both schools, which led the art critic Ignacy Matuszewski to equate the art of Burne-Jones, Watts and Rossetti with the writings of the great Polish romantic poet Juliusz Słowacki (1809–1849) in evoking tremendous but elusive feelings and moods.[17] Allusions to images produced by British Symbolists appear in a number of important works by Polish modernists, albeit transformed into a completely different language, in keeping with the mission of *Sztuka* to propagate an autonomous Polish style that could compete internationally. Wyspiański's *Apollo* (fig.8) can thus be seen as a synthesis of both Burne-Jones' *Wheel of Fortune* and *The Depths of the Sea* 1887 (Fogg Art Museum, Harvard University), its rotating personifications of planets solemnly encircling a solitary standing figure placed close to the picture plane, and Watts' *Hope* in its blue 'interior' tonality and image of a melancholy sun-god tied up with a lyre strapped to his back; but the abstract calligraphic rhythms of the composition speak an entirely fresh language. On a more general level, Watts' vitalism, or the conflation of organic processes with physical forces in his subject pictures, informs Wyspiański's epic stained-glass *God the Father – Be!* (fig.9), but in the latter the medium communicates a more electrifying message. Malczewski, a more formally academic artist than Wyspiański, was also known to incorporate references from other artists in strikingly innovative terms, a case in point being the allusion to *Hope* in the painting *On One String* of 1908 (National Museum in Warsaw) (fig.15). In this self-portrait, Malczewski creates a personal and national iconography from Watts' generic image of endurance, suggesting that the artist working under partition could only abide by one theme. In engaging with the British Symbolists in highly personal ways the Polish modernists did not perceive them as visionary dreamers in any escapist sense (a perception more common in the West), but as active agents promoting freedom of expression beyond academic conventions, enabling the viewer to attain a higher state of awareness and liberation of mind. When Wyspiański had the poet in his play *Wesele* (*The Wedding* 1901) speak to Rachela of the mystical impression she created – 'Half angel, half Madonna/ Leaning on a *chochoł*,/ like a painting by Burne-Jones' – he was not only assuming a general awareness of the artist's works, but evoked his dream-like imagery to point up the contrast between the mythic figures from Poland's past who demanded action in the present, and the lassitude and hypocrisy within contemporary society. The popularity of *Hamlet* (above all other of Shakespeare's plays) in Poland around the turn of the century was partly because the modernists identified with the protagonist because of his intellectuality, procrastination and abandonment to melancholy philosophising, qualities that merged with their appreciation for the British Symbolists.[18]

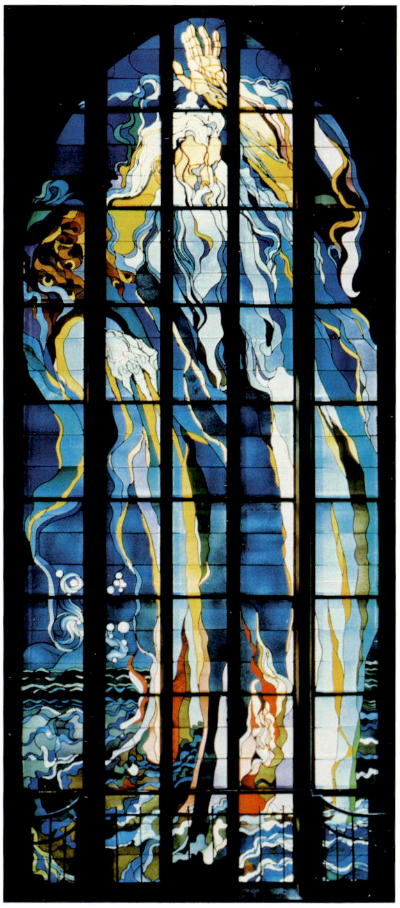

Fig.9 Stanisław Wyspiański
God the Father – Be!
1897–1904
Stained glass panel
Franciscan Church Kraków

The term 'art for art's sake', fashionable in avant-garde circles in Britain and France, was understood in Poland more in terms of a justification for rebellion against bourgeois values than as a purely aesthetic doctrine. The idea was promoted in Kraków by the cosmopolitan writer Stanisław Przybyszewski in *Życie*, and in Warsaw by the poet-critic Zenon Przesmycki, editor of *Chimera*. Polish aestheticism was informed by the writings of Pater, Algernon Charles Swinburne and Oscar Wilde, whose works were translated, texts by the latter two appearing in *Życie*. Wilde's *Salome* first appeared in Polish translation with illustrations by Beardsley in Warsaw in 1914. Whistler was another significant influence, his painted and graphic output familiar to Polish artists in Paris, and also known from the large selection of his works at the Munich Secession exhibitions of 1888, 1893 and 1895.[19] In 1904 Whistler prints were shown at the Zachęta Gallery in Warsaw, the year the artist's *Ten O'Clock Lecture* was published in Antoni Potocki's journal *Art*.

Whistler's influence can particularly be seen in the toned-down atmosphere of the portraits of Olga Boznańska (see fig.20) and the monochromatic paintings of Pankiewicz. Paintings such as Pankiewicz's *Nocturne – Swans in the Saxon Garden in Warsaw at Night* 1894 (fig.10) fuse Whistler's concept of the nocturne, which advanced the subtle dissolution and suspension of form, with the Polish idea of *nastrój* or mood, to create an indeterminate melancholy atmosphere, derived from psychological associations with the night together with a concern to question the limits of perception.

The strong sense of pattern and decoration that distinguishes the paintings of Polish modernists owed part of its inspiration to British sources. Elements of 'a Beardsleyan calligraphy' were detected by Antoni Potocki in the oeuvre of Witold Wojtkiewicz, and in Mehoffer's work in particular, the rich colour, patterning and sensuality that hallmarked Rossetti's paintings can be appreciated.[20] To give just one example, Mehoffer's *Virgin Mary c.*1890–5 (National Museum in Warsaw) bears a striking resemblance to Rossetti's *Beloved* 1865–6 (Tate) in its claustrophobic and hypnotic representation of a beauty queen surrounded by attendants. Mehoffer's *Strange Garden* (see fig.19) stands out as one of the most strikingly original works of the period, reverberating with echoes of other compositions featuring family groups bathed in sunlight, from Ford Madox Brown's *Pretty Baa-Lambs* 1851–9 (Birmingham Museums and Art Gallery) to Claude Monet's *Women in the Garden* 1866 (Musée d'Orsay) and John Singer Sargent's *Carnation, Lily, Lily, Rose* 1885–6 (Tate), but the artist transcends any such debt in conjuring up an extraordinary fairy-tale atmosphere through a seemingly bizarre blend of decorative stylisation and *plein-air* realism. Although the child motif appears markedly in the work of European Symbolists and Post-Impressionists around 1900, it took on an ambivalent range of meanings within partitioned Poland, being a gesture of hope for the future, yet also forming an iconography of despair, a poignant reminder of the failure of

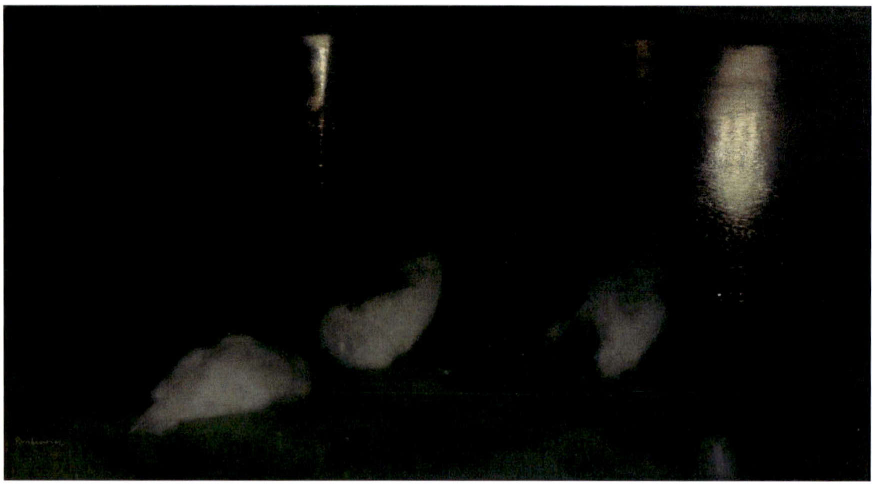

Fig.10 Józef Pankiewicz
Nocturne – Swans in the Saxon Garden in Warsaw at Night
1894
Oil on canvas
86 x 151
National Museum Warsaw

successive generations to achieve liberation and maturation. Mehoffer's representation of his naked son in *Strange Garden* conveys the innocence and wonderment of childhood, fuelling the political theme of the child as the harbinger of national regeneration expressed in other works. By contrast, Wojtkiewicz's grotesque depiction of infants in disorientating environments suggests decadence and entrapment. Influenced in part by the fantasy stories of Oscar Wilde, in the context of partitioned Poland, Wojtkiewicz's disturbing expressionistic images assert a mood of impotence and frustrated growth.

Probably the most productive interaction with the Pre-Raphaelites concerned the theories of William Morris and John Ruskin. Overlooking the metaphysical aspect of the latter's writings, Ruskin's ideas were often viewed as interchangeable with those of Morris, which had the effect of turning him into a precursor of the Arts and Crafts Movement in combining ideas of beauty and function, and upholding craftsmanship against mass production. Parallels can be drawn between Arts and Crafts philosophy and that of *Sztuka* in that both groups rejected hierarchical distinctions between the arts in promoting the democratisation of culture. Given the relationship between these ideas and the cultural policies of the burgeoning Socialist movement, it was the designer Walter Crane, an active participant within international Socialism, who attained a unique status in Central Europe. His works were exhibited at the Lvov Municipal Museum of Industry in 1895, and at the Museum of Applied Art in Budapest in 1900, the latter event accompanied by numerous publications on the artist. Within Poland it was the Socialist magazine *Naprzód* (Forward) that propagated the utopian postcards Crane designed for activist purposes around 1897, such as *The Triumph of Labour* in the present display (fig.11), which harmonises pastoral with allegorical imagery to celebrate wage workers of all nations.

Enthusiasm for the writings of Ruskin and Morris peaked around 1900, especially within Young Poland, which adopted the writers' critique of

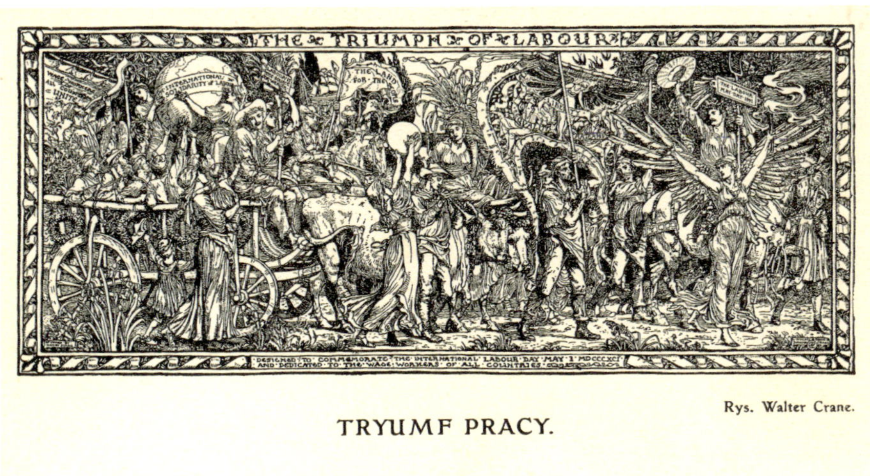

Fig.11 Walter Crane
The Triumph of Labour
1897
Zincograph on paper
9 x 14
The Sosenko Family Archives and Collections

capitalism as the cause of division in labour, and of commerce as detrimental to beauty and integrity in design. Morris' example of working across different genres was a source of inspiration to both Wyspiański and Mehoffer, who similarly operated as designers and decorators of medieval churches (see figs.9 and 18). It was through the influence of Morris and Ruskin that Bonawentura Lenart studied at Camberwell School of Art with the idea of book reform in mind, and the stage designer Karol Frycz came to study at Hubert von Herkomer's Art School in Bushey, west of London, around 1904. Nevertheless, the very personal adaptation of Arts and Crafts philosophy by Polish designers was countered by accusations that in elevating medievalism above the machine, British designers aimed at a spurious utopian goal. It was Morris' biographer Winiarski who criticised the Pre-Raphaelites for looking to the past, contending: 'It is only in the environment of a carefree democracy and under its influence that the personalities of the Pre-Raphaelites became stultified.'[21] He went on to claim that any aspiring national school should create new forms that projected into the future, a statement which could be interpreted as a covert appeal made under Russian partition and censorship that the turbulent political predicament of Poland be turned to its advantage by channelling the creative impulse to the present and future, rather than retreating into the past, as was the risk for designers working in a seemingly more peaceful context.

Despite the equivocation surrounding Ruskin's and Morris' social ideas of art, it would be true to say that the Arts and Crafts Movement had an important influence in Poland, particularly in Kraków, situated in the relatively liberal Austro-Hungarian Empire. As early as 1868 the doctor and philanthropist Adrian Baraniecki opened the Industrial Museum at Kraków, based on the South Kensington model in London, with the objective of promoting design reform and reinvigorating industry. The Polish Applied Art Society, established in Kraków in 1901, which developed from this, acknowledged Ruskin and Morris in its aim of nurturing a Polish national style in design. It was the Arts and Crafts interest in vernacular traditions that encouraged the expansion of interest in folk art within Poland, the ideal of a national style based on folk traditions finding complete expression in the work of Stanisław Witkiewicz and his Zakopane style, which drew on the crafts produced by the inhabitants of the Podhale region in southern Poland (see fig.14). Witkiewicz referred to Ruskin as a 'kindred spirit', and seemingly tried to solicit his support for the idea of a Zakopane style as representing an ideal community of craftsmen. The daughter of the historic novelist Henryk Sienkiewicz apparently sent some photographs of houses and objects produced in the Zakopane style to Ruskin, who affirmed 'the originality of this "Polish style", and regretted that because of his old age he could not undertake such a long journey and see the artefacts for himself'.[22] Walter Crane, who travelled twice in Central Europe, in 1890 (Bohemia) and 1900

(Hungary), saw in the provincial communities he encountered the simple and dignified life of a pre-industrialised world. Joseph Conrad's sojourn in Zakopane in 1914 gave impetus to his plans for direct action in Britain in support of Polish interests, as expressed in his essay 'Poland Revisited', published in 1921. Whereas in Central Europe, British art was regarded as an example of how manufacture could invigorate national identity, for Britons alert to the culture of Central Europe, countries such as Poland maintained the moral communitarian values of the Middle Ages and in so doing represented a utopia unattainable in industrialised societies.

With these examples in mind, one could argue that both nations viewed each other from opposing perspectives, Britain finding in the remoter regions of Europe societies unblemished by technology and progress, the Poles looking to Britain as the leading light of modernisation. Although this simplifies the connections explored in this publication and overlooks the different strands of interchange, there certainly existed a tendency for each to mythologise the other, which allowed for mutual idealisation. Although Young Poland had little impact in Britain, the devotion Paderewski received in Britain matches the mystic reverence Burne-Jones and Watts were accorded in Poland, all regarded as vital agents inspiring transformation within the individual as well as society at large. Looking back from the twenty-first century, the Polish modernists' dialogue with the Pre-Raphaelites provides an important testimony to the influence the later phase of the movement had beyond Britain around 1900. Through Polish eyes the Pre-Raphaelites' quest for beauty was not just an expression of disillusionment with their rapidly changing society, or retreat into a hermetic world of symbols, but an affirmation that the creation of a truly modern, national and democratic art offered the possibility of a better world.

The Young Poland Movement: Art, Nation, Modernity

PIOTR KOPSZAK AND ANDRZEJ SZCZERSKI

At the beginning of the twentieth century, Polish art enjoyed a period of extraordinary intensity and energy. Its youthful dynamism was clearly recognised by contemporaries, who coined the term 'Young Poland' ('*Młoda Polska*'). It was part of a spectacular rebirth of national culture in the face of a troubled political situation. Poland had endured a century-long enslavement under the rule of three neighbouring foreign powers – Austria, Prussia (later Germany) and Russia – which partitioned the country at the end of the eighteenth century. This action effectively brought to an end the existence of the kingdom based on the union between Poland and Lithuania, known as the Rzeczpospolita Obojga Narodów (Polish-Lithuanian Commonwealth), founded at the end of the fourteenth century. Despite various efforts to save the country, with wide-ranging political and economic reforms as well as military resistance, each partitioning power between 1772 and 1795 incorporated into its own state different regions of Rzeczpospolita. Prussia took the western provinces, including the city of Poznań and the Baltic coast, and Austria the south-eastern part, including Kraków and Lvov.

Russia secured control over the largest territories, including roughly the present-day states of Latvia, Lithuania, Belarus, and central and western Ukraine, and as a result of the Napoleonic Wars in 1815 it expanded into the Polish heartland with the capital in Warsaw, hitherto controlled by Prussia. Subsequent Polish uprisings in the nineteenth century were brutally suppressed, and culture provided the only relatively liberal platform for the expression of national sentiment and debate concerning the future fate of the country.[1] This chapter in Polish history ended in 1918, when in the aftermath of the First World War Poland regained its independence. Its first Prime Minister was to be the pianist and politician Ignacy Jan Paderewski, well known on the London art scene and painted by Edward Burne-Jones and other British artists (see figs.2–3 and Alison Smith's essay in this volume).

Until the middle of the nineteenth century, Polish culture was dominated by literature. This prompted Julian Klaczko, one of the most acute critics of the period, to state in 1857 that Poles were not capable of producing their own national visual arts and should concentrate on their unquestionable talents for the 'word'.[2] However, from the 1860s the situation changed significantly, due to the emergence of a new generation of artists educated both at home and abroad, mainly in the art academies and schools of Munich, Paris and St Petersburg.

Of these the best known was the academic painter Jan Matejko, based in

Kraków. His large-scale canvases, representing scenes from Polish history in an expressionist and sentimental style, received recognition not only at home but also abroad, especially in France. His *chef-d'oeuvre*, *The Battle of Grunwald* 1878 (fig.12), was exhibited in Kraków, Warsaw, Vienna, St Petersburg, Berlin, Lvov, Budapest and Paris between 1878 and 1880. Matejko not only provided Polish culture with a powerful visual language equal to that of its literature, but also paved the way for the phenomenal growth of painting around 1900, which was largely dominated by his own students from the newly founded School of Fine Arts in Kraków (opened in 1873 and raised to the status of Academy in 1900).

In Matejko, the Polish public saw the ideal 'artist-prophet', destined to rule over the national soul. Such a prophet figure could in times of political downfall perform the role of a national 'interrex'. In October 1878, a month after the *The Battle of Grunwald* was first exhibited, the authorities of Kraków bestowed a symbolic sceptre on Matejko with which he could rule over Polish art, in recognition of his status in the public life of his effectively non-existent country.[3]

In the early twentieth century, the Austrian partition of Poland, with its two major cities of Lvov and Kraków, enjoyed great cultural autonomy due to the internal reforms in the Hapsburg Empire introduced in the 1860s. Known as Galicia, the area quickly became the centre of national culture, focused on the ancient capital of the Polish kingdom, Kraków, with its active artistic milieu. The Viennese Ministry of Religion and Education also played an animating role by financing Kraków's art institutions. A significant contribution was also made both by Warsaw, thanks to activities of the Warsaw School of Fine Arts and the Society for the Encouragement of Fine Arts (*Zachęta*), and by Vilnius, where artistic activity started to gain momentum at the very end of the nineteenth century.

Fig.12 Jan Matejko
The Battle of Grunwald
1878
Oil on canvas
426 x 987
National Museum Warsaw

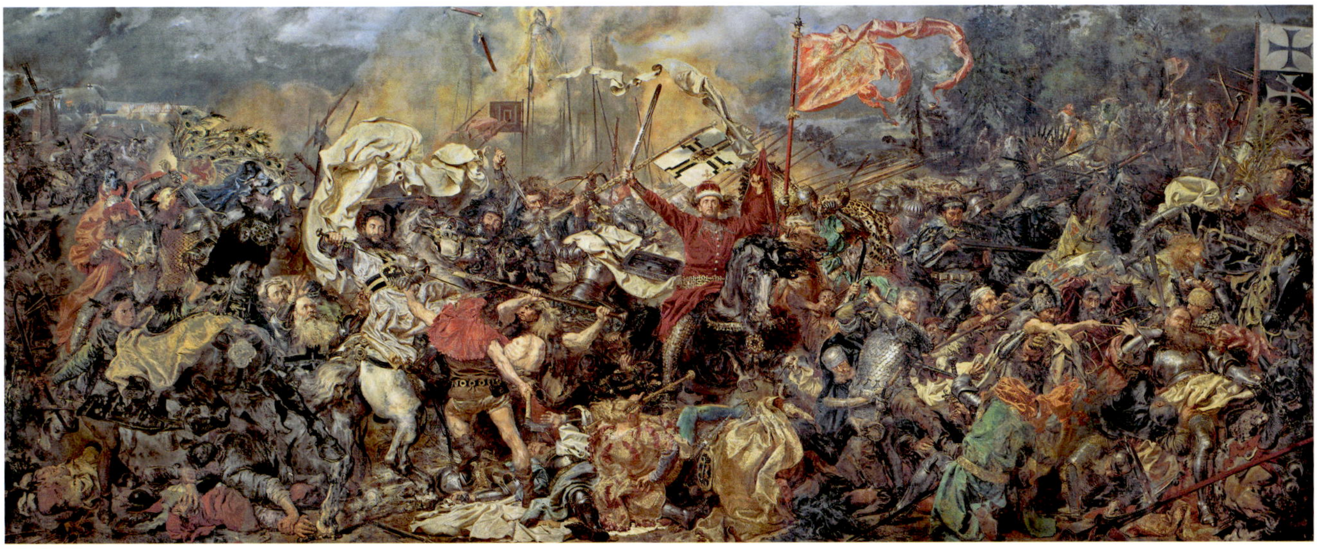

Thanks to this diversity, artistic life in Poland flourished across political borders, and focused on various themes concerning the new art and its role in national history. The issue of the revival of national art had long been a major concern among artists, yet it also needs to be seen in the context of the other significant problems of modernisation and the emergence of a new concept of the human being. For artists who reached maturity around 1900, the 'national' question appeared in the context of neo-Romantic ideals, in which the evocation of a glorious national past overlapped with the new cult of individuality as well as ideas about primordial communities defined by common mythical origins. Romantic ideals also influenced the renewed interest in nature and mysticism.[4]

At the turn of the twentieth century the debate arose among artists concerning the search for a distinctive Polish national style. Hopes for an assertion of national identity found their expression in paintings and sculptures related to Polish history and national myths, and the Romantic idea of Polish messianism. These works implied that the sufferings of Poles had a deeper, spiritual meaning and served to redeem Europe. Poland appeared as the 'Christ of Nations', modelled on the symbolism of the sacrifice of Jesus Christ: in romantic literature for example, contemporary Poland was compared to the crucified Jesus Christ, especially by Mickiewicz. In the fine arts, the religious iconography of crucifixion appeared in works dedicated to national uprisings, and the sacrifice of national heroes, or in visionary works, such as Wyspiański's *Polonia* (fig.13).[5]

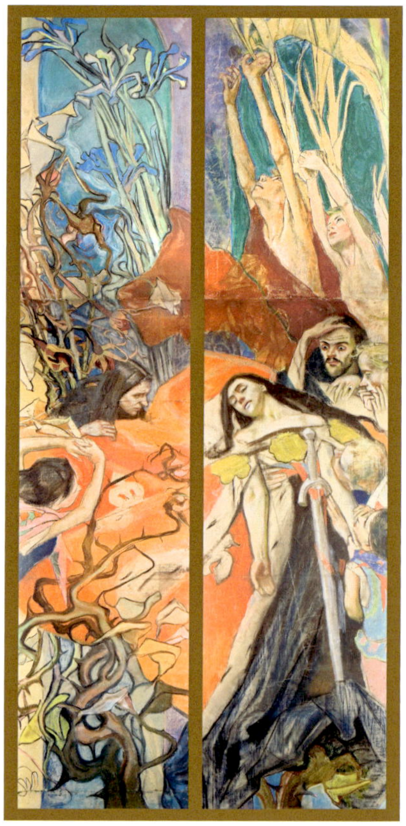

Fig.13 Stanisław Wyspiański
Polonia
1893–4
Sketch for stained glass; pastel, paper
320 x 193
National Museum Kraków

Issues of the 'Polishness' of particular landscapes or regions were also raised, resulting, for example, in the new cult of admiration for the Tatra Mountains, the highest part of the Carpathian range, in southern Poland and their indigenous highlander population. Artists were eager to pave the way for the national revival both in their art and way of life. Three eminent representatives of a Cracovian cultural scene, including the painter and designer Stanisław Wyspiański and the poet Lucjan Rydel, married peasant women from local villages in a radical gesture against the social conventions and historic divisions within Polish society.

National sentiment also lay behind the foundation of various concepts of national style in architecture and interior design, based on vernacular buildings and decorations, as well as folk art. The greatest preference among Poles in all the three partitions was for the Zakopane style, invented in the 1890s by the painter and art critic Stanisław Witkiewicz, who found his inspiration in the material culture of highlanders living in the area of the Tatra Mountains known as Podhale.

Witkiewicz named the style after the principal village of the region. He believed that local highlanders, known as the Górale, preserved in their building techniques, decorative arts, language and music, the essence of early Polish culture, untouched by foreign influences, which could thus serve as a source of contemporary national revival. In his designs for houses and interiors, including his masterpiece the *House under the Firs*, for the Pawlikowski family in Zakopane (1897) (fig.14), Witkiewicz freely adapted and refined the construction and ornamental patterns of the highlanders' buildings – drawing also on other sources such as contemporary National Romantic architecture in Europe and America, but also on traditional Siberian carpentry, which he saw while in exile there – to create a new model of a Polish house.[6]

At the same time he wanted to prove that the peasant class could be the source of national revival and solidarity. Witkiewicz tried to export his style beyond the Podhale region and, thanks to sympathetic patrons, he was commissioned to design and occasionally build Zakopane-style houses in provincial areas of Poland and Lithuania, as well as in major cities such as Warsaw. One of Witkiewicz's most ardent supporters was Franciszek Mączyński, who in 1901 presented a design for a city built entirely in the Zakopane style; this however remained a symbol of unrealised national utopia.

In Lvov architects such as Jan and Alfred Zachariewicz and Tadeusz Obmiński designed their own version of a vernacular national style, based on the heritage of the Eastern Carpathians. This included references to the culture of the local highlanders of that region, who are known as Huzuls. Yet they could not compete with the national impact of Witkiewicz's ideas, and their endeavours remained confined to eastern Galicia.[7]

At the same time there was an intensification of the international contacts between Polish and other European artists, as if the newly redefined national identity helped to establish contacts with other fellow nations and their cultures. Significantly, this emerging network encompassed representatives of cultures previously perceived as marginal to Europe, not only those close at hand like modern Czech artists, but also further afield, for example in Scandinavia and Britain. This artistic contact led to the creation of a new model of European identity, based on the multiple centres of regional and national importance involved in a mutual exchange of thoughts and ideas. This was in contrast to a Europe hitherto dominated by one cultural centre, in Paris, which provided a single and homogeneous definition of Europe.

Parallels between Polish and British painting and literature were discovered by artists and critics around 1900, thanks to *The Studio* magazine and the Parisian fame of Edward Burne-Jones and Dante Gabriel Rossetti, and resulted in a new dynamism in art. A new model of internationalism thus emerged in Europe, which embraced direct contacts between cultures previously largely unknown to each other. Just as the art of the Pre-Raphaelites was understood in Poland as an example of a national English style, so it could also have been perceived as having the same goals as Polish artists involved in the search for 'Polishness', both in form and in content.

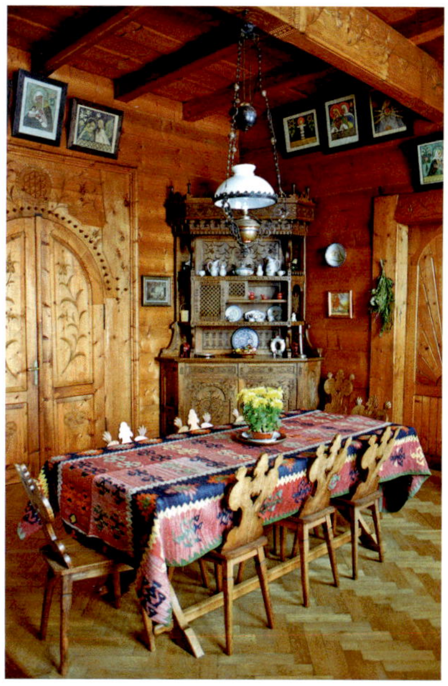

Fig.14 Stanisław Witkiewicz
The House under the Firs, Zakopane,
1897
Interior view

Paradoxically, the search for national uniqueness could result in the appreciation of diverse cultures and the importance of stimulating contact between them against the divisions imposed by political and economic barriers.[8] In Poland, a country of various nationalities and religions, dramatically divided between foreign powers, this urge to find new channels of communication was particularly urgent. It should be noted that Poland was also the home of Ludwik Zamenhof, born in the city of Białystok, who in the 1880s invented the language of Esperanto, based on various European languages in order to facilitate the communication between different nations and enhance international cooperation.

One of the most characteristic traits of Polish *fin-de-siècle* art was its tendency towards Symbolism. Artists and writers expressed their ideas with elaborate references to national culture and history, but also to contemporary debates about Nietzschean and Bergsonian concepts of mankind and the world.[9] This flourishing culture of Symbolism can be explained by the intimate bond of visual arts and poetry, common in Europe at the time. In the Polish context the revival of interest in the poetry of three key early nineteenth-century Romantic poets, Adam Mickiewicz, Juliusz Słowacki and Zygmunt Krasiński, was central. Their work, of unparalleled richness of language and refinement of style, endowed Polish poetry with a prophetic dimension that looked to the future rebirth of the country.

The linguistic metaphors employed by these poets seemed to translate easily into visual language, and hence shaped the imagination of subsequent generations of artists. In the 1890s the forgotten Romantic poet Cyprian Kamil Norwid was rediscovered. A poet of extraordinary vision, Norwid was also a draughtsman and painter, and hence a role model artist-poet for the exponents of Polish Symbolism. Several famous painters such as Jacek Malczewski, wrote often underrated poetry, but in the case of Stanisław Wyspiański, his literature, including poetry and theatre plays, won him a recognition equal to his visual artwork. In the context of the literary interest of Polish Symbolism, it should not be surprising that the Pre-Raphaelite Brotherhood, especially Rossetti, whose works had been translated into Polish, should have appeared as kindred spirits.

The ancestry of Polish Symbolism can be traced back to works by artists associated with the Polish artists' colony in Munich. They were graduates and students of the Munich Academy who began to settle in the Bavarian capital in the second half of the nineteenth century. In the 1880s, Witold Pruszkowski began to paint nature with a sense of Symbolist *stimmung* or mood, and his landscapes were often inhabited by mythological figures.[10]

The most outstanding figure among these proto-Symbolists was Adam Chmielowski. In his early career, Chmielowski painted refined emotional landscapes, but later his interest in idealism combined with social sensitivity, pushed him towards the service of the poor and the foundation of a new

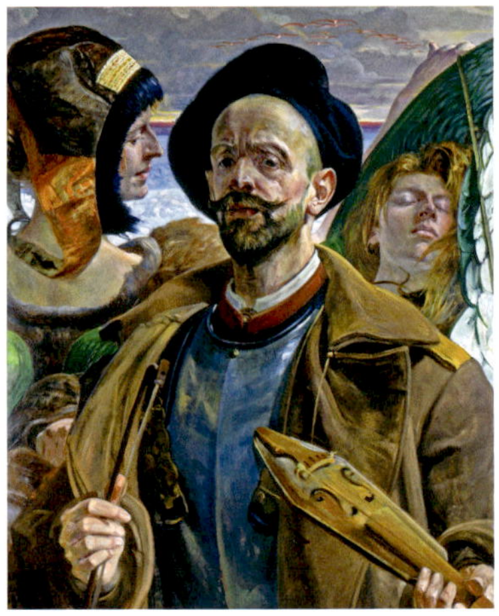

Fig.15 Jacek Malczewski
On One String (Self-portrait)
1908
Oil on carton
92 x 73
National Museum Warsaw

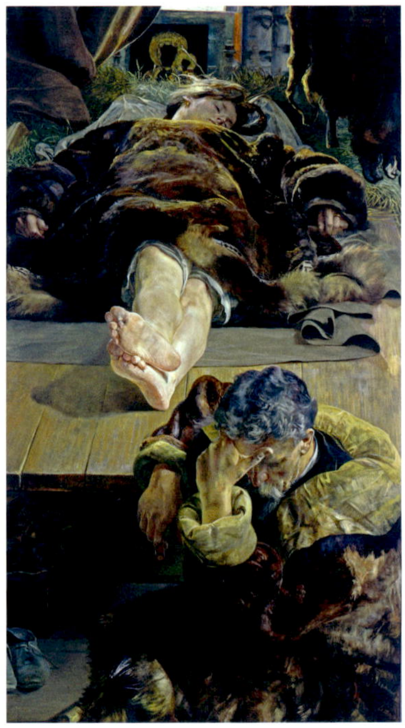

Fig.16 Jacek Malczewski
The Death of Ellenai
1907
Oil on canvas
208 x 114
Property of the Raczyński Foundation at the National Museum Poznań

charitable Catholic order. Already venerated during his lifetime, he was canonised by the Roman Catholic Church in 1989.[11]

But it was Jacek Malczewski, Matejko's student and a notable eccentric, who directed Polish art firmly towards Symbolism in the 1890s. In his paintings angels and nymphs are placed alongside human beings, and his portrait sitters are always accompanied by mythological figures appropriate to their personalities. Malczewski belonged to a generation that was deeply wounded by the political repercussions after the failed January Uprising against Russia in 1863–4. Polish insurgents, among them the Malczewski family, were sent into long years of Siberian exile. This provided the young artist with a powerful subject, which he painted frequently during the 1860s.[12] While painting the enslavement of Polish exiles, he discarded the historicist style of Matejko and accepted the new visual language of French Realism. This led to a major Symbolist shift in his career, in the mid-1890s, when he executed his two masterpieces, *Melancholy* 1894 and *The Vicious Circle* 1895–7. In both works, the figure of a painter is surrounded by a crowd, seen as if in a vision, composed of Polish insurgents, as well as figures symbolising the forces of Eros and Thanatos, joined in a ritual dance. In this context, the artist depicted holds a privileged but challenging position; he is the source of a vision concerning national revival, but is also responsible for its future use and appeal.

Malczewski found his favourite source of inspiration in Słowacki's poem about Siberian exiles, *Anhelli* (1838), which dealt with the first wave of expulsions after the November Uprising against Russia in 1830–1. Malczewski saw this Romantic story as a symbol of sacrifice for freedom, which bestowed on the suffering Polish exiles a sense of sublime dignity. He was particularly obsessed with a scene in Słowacki's poem *The Death of Ellenai*. The poem deals with the imagined journey through Siberia of young Anhelli, the son of a Polish exile, where he discovers the misery of Polish exiles and their sacrifices, but also the devastating effects of slavery. In the final part of the poem Anhelli's companion Ellenai dies, leaving him alone, her soul taken away by the angel of exiles, Eloe. As the contemporary critic Bolesław Prus, writing about the 1883 version of the painting *The Death of Ellenai*, put it, the artist managed to show the existential truth of a loss of a beloved human being (fig.16).[13]

Malczewski revisited the Ellenai death theme after the 1905 Revolution, which in the Russian partition resembled earlier Polish national uprisings, enhancing the contemporary relevance of Romantic symbols. Reenacting the Romantic slogans and commitments concerning the fight for independence, led to a renewed interest in early nineteenth century literature and music, and to the image of the warrior hero, ready to sacrifice himself for national community and the future resurrection of the independent country. In the four new versions of the subject, the irrational aspect of the heroine's death

Fig.17 Jacek Malczewski
Eloe with Ellenai
1907–09
Oil on canvas
218 x 129
National Museum Poznań

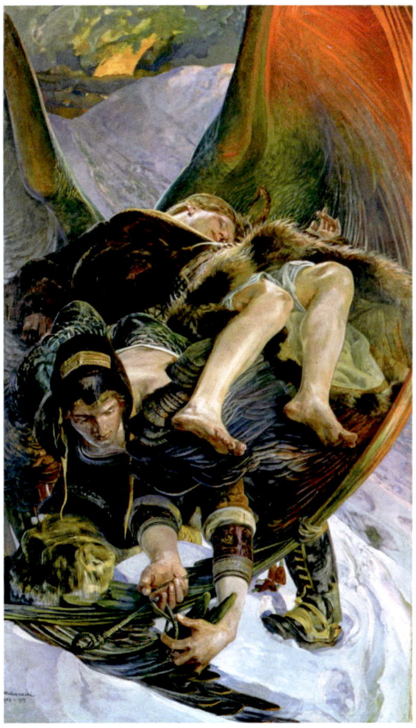

prevailed. In 1907–9, instead of a realistic rendering, Malczewski painted *Eloe with Ellenai* with an angel carrying Ellenai's body to heaven, clearly referring to the Christian iconography of the Assumption (fig.17).

Another major representative of the Polish art scene around 1900 was Józef Mehoffer, the descendant of an Austrian family that became naturalised Poles and settled in Kraków in the mid-nineteenth century. His works were particularly well known for their attractive aesthetic qualities, based on colour harmonies and ornamental arabesques, and were influenced by contemporary Art Nouveau ideas. Throughout his life Mehoffer turned to the Roman Catholic religion as a source of inspiration, and his profound knowledge of Christian iconography was unique among his contemporaries. He executed numerous church decorations in all three provinces of the partitioned Poland; however, his most famous commission was from the Swiss city of Fribourg, where he designed a complete set of stained-glass windows for the Church of St Nicholas (1895–1936).[14]

At home, Mehoffer won great prestige for his decoration of the Polish Pantheon, the medieval Cathedral on Wawel Hill in Kraków. He designed several stained-glass windows there illustrating the themes of suffering and redemption, as seen in for example *Geniuses of Sorrow* at Wawel Hill Cathedral (1904–11) (fig.18). His earlier decorations of the Cathedral Treasury (1901–1902) were a source of intense debate, with the traditionalists considering the boldly modern works of Mehoffer to be inappropriate for a medieval ecclesiastical building. Among Mehoffer's rare decorations of secular spaces, his work for the Chamber of Industry and Commerce in Kraków (1905–1906) stands out. In the Chamber's debating hall, the artist implemented the *Gesamtkunstwerk* idea (where all the branches of fine arts and design are united to produce one overwhelming effect), designing the whole interior, including the furniture and wall paintings, in a style inspired by vernacular and folk-art motifs.[15]

Mehoffer, who for the greater part of his life taught painting at Kraków Academy, is best remembered for his paintings, especially *Strange Garden* 1903, the widely acknowledged icon of the Polish *fin de siècle* (fig.19). The painting is a family portrait, featuring his wife Jadwiga and their little son, accompanied by a maid dressed in a folk costume. The garden turns into a medieval 'Hortus Deliciarum' (Garden of Delights), in which the precise depiction of plants recalls the meticulous realism of medieval painting, also associated with the works of the Pre-Raphaelite Brotherhood. The uncanny effect of dream-like verisimilitude is emphasised by a dragonfly that hovers above the group, and looks like a magnified precious Art Nouveau jewel, both menacing and intriguing.

The Symbolist mood in Mehoffer's work recalls that of James Abbott McNeill Whistler, who was a significant source of inspiration for Polish *fin-de-siècle* painting. Whistler's influence is especially evident in works by

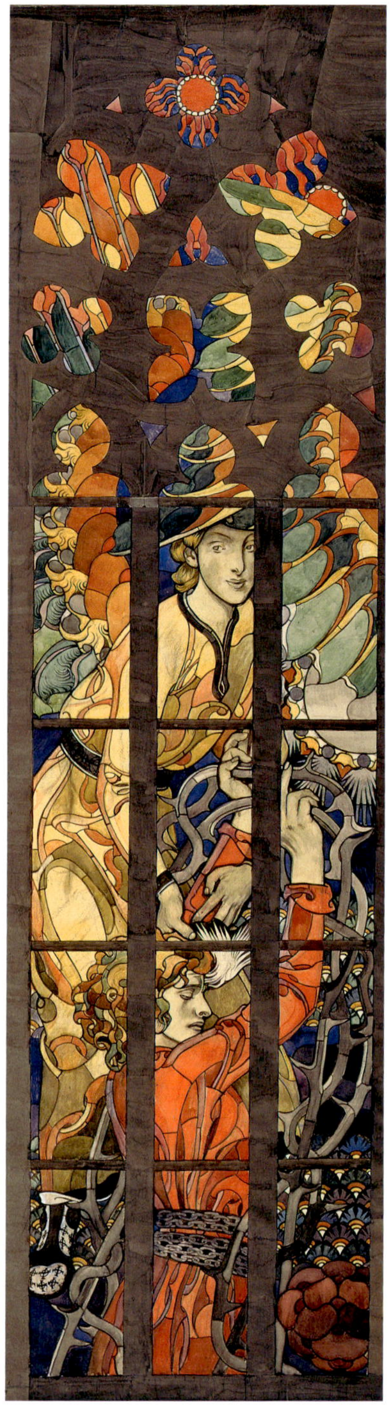

Fig.18 Józef Mehoffer
Genius of Sorrow I
1911
Fragment of the stained-glass window, watercolour, india ink, paper on canvas
529 x 153
National Museum Warsaw

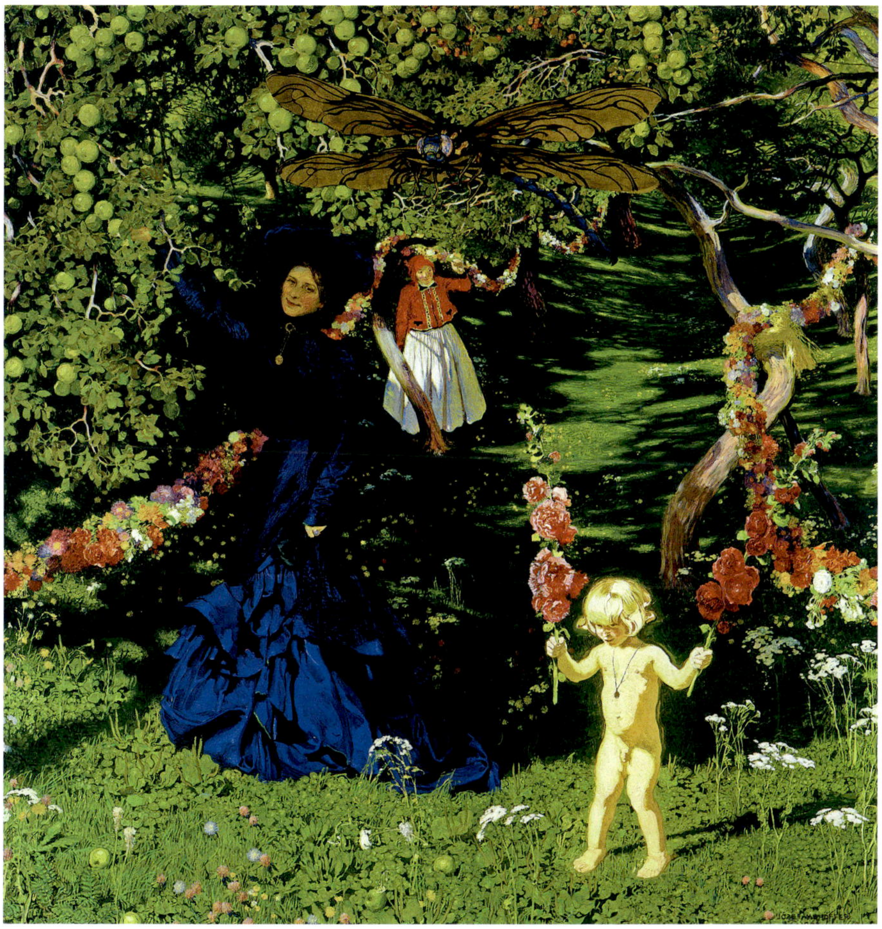

Fig.19 Józef Mehoffer
Strange Garden
1902–1903
Oil on canvas
217 x 208
National Museum Warsaw

Fig.20 Olga Boznańska
Portrait of a Boy in a Grammar School Uniform
c.1890
Oil on canvas
180 x 100
National Museum Warsaw

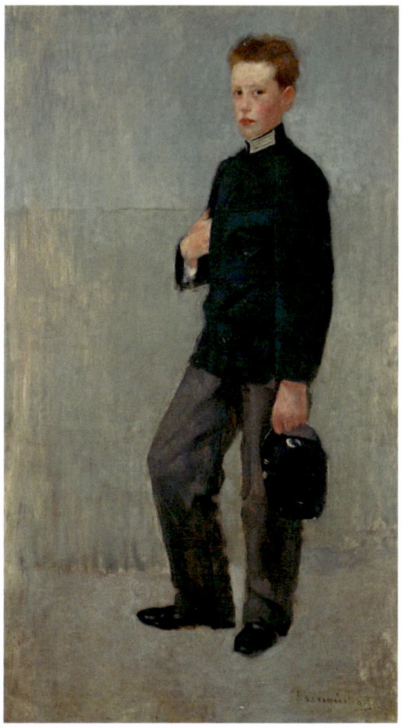

Olga Boznańska and Józef Pankiewicz, both of whom were active, mostly in Paris, at the end of the 1890s. Boznańska was born in Kraków, educated in private schools there and in Munich, and quickly became one of the most prolific and active European women artists. Her portraits were highly regarded for their Symbolist qualities, and contemporary reviewers like William Ritter compared her works to the Symbolist poems of Maurice Maeterlinck. Her *Portrait of a Boy in a Grammar School Uniform* c.1890 (fig.20) illustrates her refined painterly technique, as well as her interest in the psychology of adolescence and her obvious fascination with Whistler's compositions.[16]

Pankiewicz first went to Paris in 1889, where he quickly became infatuated with Impressionism. Upon his return to Warsaw in January 1890, he presented his Impressionist works, together with works by his colleague, another early Polish Impressionist, Władysław Podkowiński. Their exhibition sparked heated discussions in the Polish press about Impressionism, in which the enemies of the new style appeared to prevail. As a result Pankiewicz soon changed his style completely and moved towards a sombre and poetic version of Symbolism.

His *Nocturne – Swans in the Saxon Garden in Warsaw at Night* 1894 (see fig.10) was painted after reading the poem *Le vierge, le vivace et le bel aujourd'hui* by Stéphane Mallarmé. It includes the same use of almost abstract, illegible shapes made by paint on canvas as Whistler's own *Nocturnes.*[17] The style of refined elegance, the emphasis on the cult of the individual and the aristocratic exclusivity to be found in Pankiewicz's painting were typical features of the work by the artists who in 1897 established the Polish counterpart of the Viennese Secession – the *Sztuka* (Art) secessionist society in Kraków, although the society cherished diversity and pronounced its commitment to the true value of art as a whole rather than particular currents.

The Whistlerian musical aesthetic also influenced the Lithuanian Kazimierz Stabrowski who was the first Director of the Warsaw School of Fine Arts. In Warsaw, Stabrowski was a teacher of Mikalojus Konstantinas Čiurlionis, a Lithuanian composer and one of the pioneers of abstraction, who took up painting to create visual compositions based on musical harmonies.

The Warsaw School of Fine Arts gained a reputation as a leading institution of higher education in the Russian Empire. A series of postcards designed by its professors and students in 1905 reflects the typical folk inspirations of the time, as well as a clearly visible drive towards abstraction (fig.21). Stabrowski was also admired as a portrait painter of exquisite elegance. His *Portrait of the Artist's Wife* c.1907 (fig.22) in which the subject is shown in regal, yet relaxed pose, bears some resemblance to contemporary portraits by John Singer Sargent.

At the turn of the twentieth century, idealism in Polish art found its counterpart in the rise of naturalism and its new modernist interpretation, shaped decisively by writer Stanisław Przybyszewski and his theory of 'psychic naturalism'. Przybyszewski's position as a protagonist of the Berlin avant garde, together with his tormented visions of sexuality and human introspection, and his early awareness of the career of Edvard Munch, were very well known in Poland. When Przybyszewski arrived in Kraków in 1898 to work as editor of the modernist journal *Życie*, he was immediately baptised as the leader of a new decadent movement.

Przybyszewski's ideas found an echo in the expressionist works of Wojciech Weiss. Weiss was the early follower of Edvard Munch, long before the German expressionists, a painter of spiritual landscapes, expressionist nudes, explorer of adolescent dreams and a gifted portraitist. He was fascinated with the dynamism of the forces of nature and the exploration of human nature.[18]

In the works of Witold Wojtkiewicz, who was also seen as working under the spell of Przybyszewski, expressionism turned grotesque. His paintings, and drawings in particular, demonstrate exceptional expressionist technique

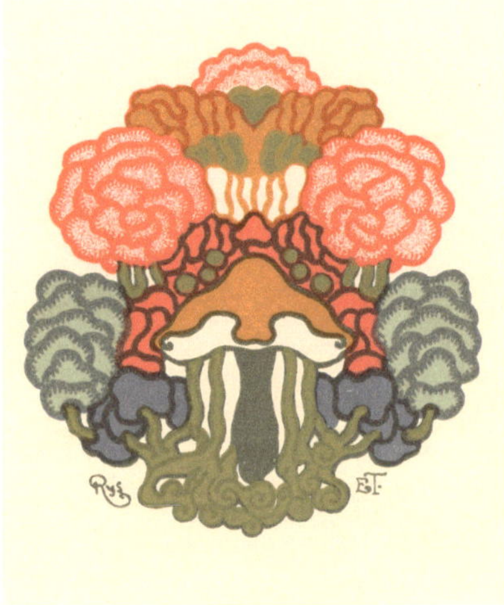

Fig.21 Edward Trojanowski
Postcard with a Decorative Motif
c.1905
Lithography on cardboard
9 x 14
The Sosenko Family Archives and Collections

Fig.22 Kazimierz Stabrowski
Portrait of the Artist's wife
c.1907
Oil on canvas
160 x 98
National Museum Warsaw

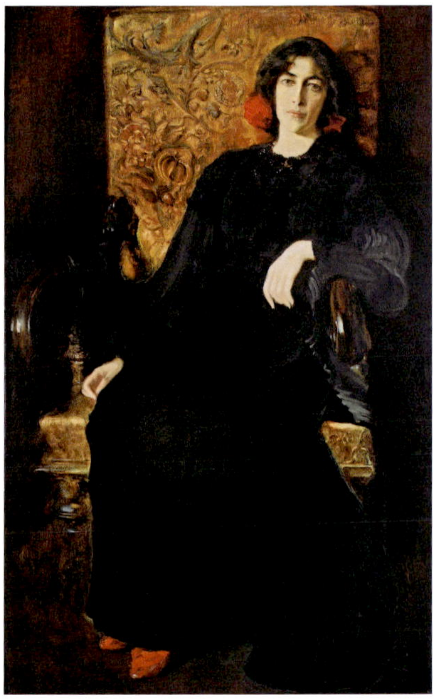

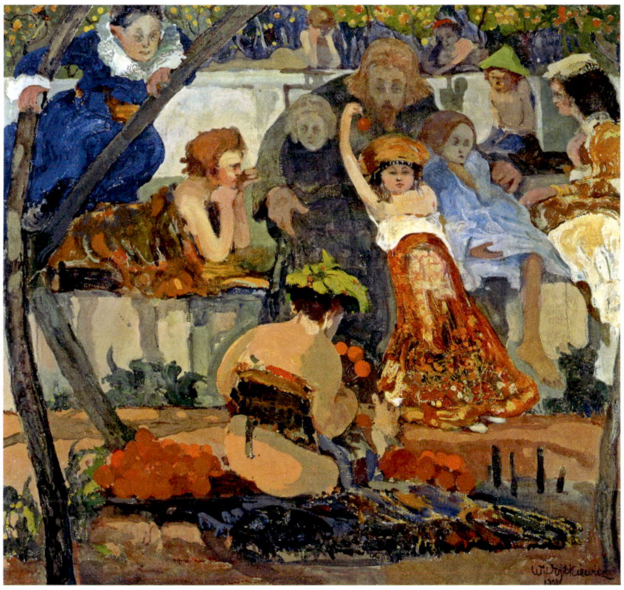

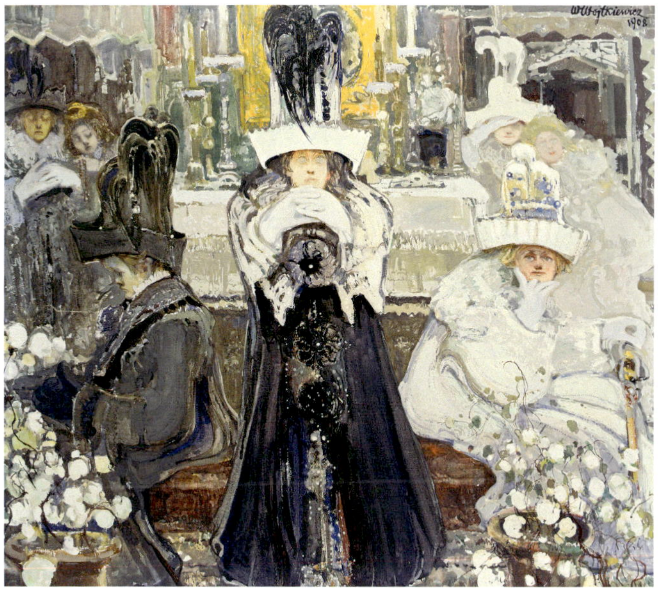

and attention to detail. Significantly, the critic Antoni Potocki compared the artist Witold Wojtkiewicz to Aubrey Beardsley. Indeed, they shared not only a bitter view of the society in which they lived, but also an infinite devotion to their imaginative art – not to mention their dandyism. Wojtkiewicz peopled his canvases with images of weak misfits unable to cope with everyday life: children who grew up prematurely, and old people performing actions whose meaning remains obscure to the viewer. His world was the never-ending comedy of human life, and he titled his painting cycles *Tragicomical Sketches* 1904, *Ceremonies* 1908 or *Circus* 1905–7. In these works humans are given a status equal to that of dolls and marionettes, their lives split between the grotesque and the sublime.[19]

Wojtkiewicz also collaborated with the satirical journals of Kraków and frequented the famous cabaret the Little Green Balloon (*Zielony Balonik*), both of which brought him into contact with the city's avant garde. The cabaret performed a crucial role in Kraków's artistic life around 1900. It was the bohemian domain where new ideas concerning art and society were discussed. It was also an important meeting place for a variety of artists and designers. Among these was Kazimierz Sichulski, a successful painter and cartoonist, known for the decorative delicacy of his drawings. Born in Lvov, where he was mostly active as an artist, he became fascinated with the art and customs of the Huzuls, the highlanders of the Eastern Carpathians, but also with the idea of the brotherhood of the three historic nations of Poland, Lithuania and Ruthenia (Ukraine), which he illustrated in the triptych *Holy Family* 1913 (fig.26). Sichulski's *Angel* (fig.25) shows a refined composition, based on the correspondence between ornamental patterns and the gentle figure of a young girl, inspired by a Huzul model. Her angelic wings, composed of peacock feathers, are reminiscent of a favourite motif of the

Fig.23 Witold Wojtkiewicz
Christ and the Children
1908
Oil on canvas
65 x 70
National Museum Warsaw

Fig.24 Witold Wojtkiewicz
Meditations
1908
Oil on canvas
80 x 90
National Museum Kraków

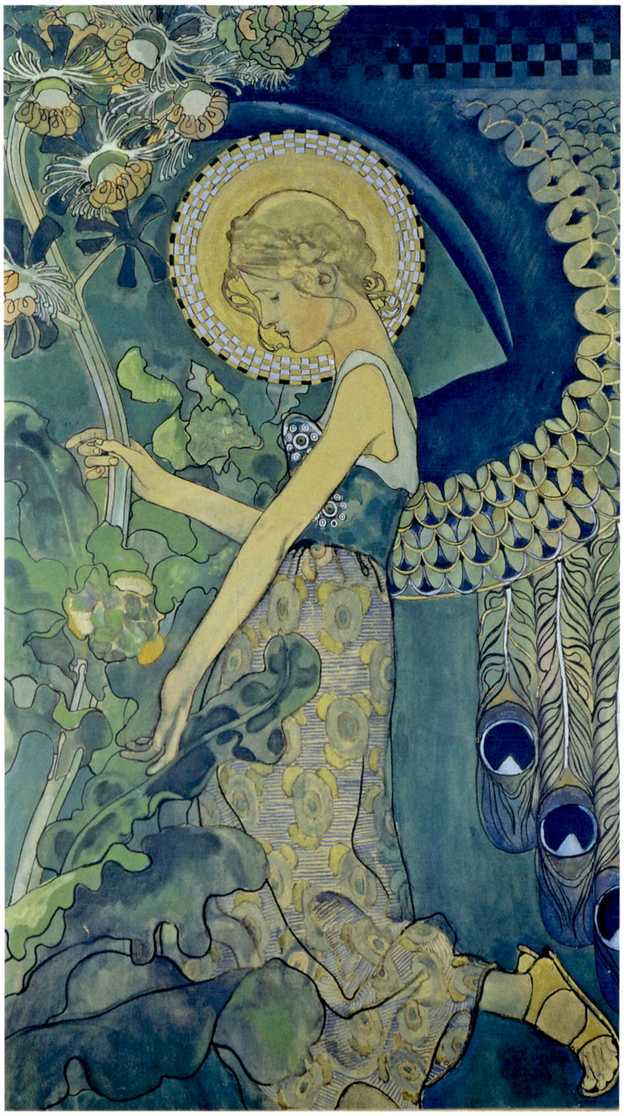

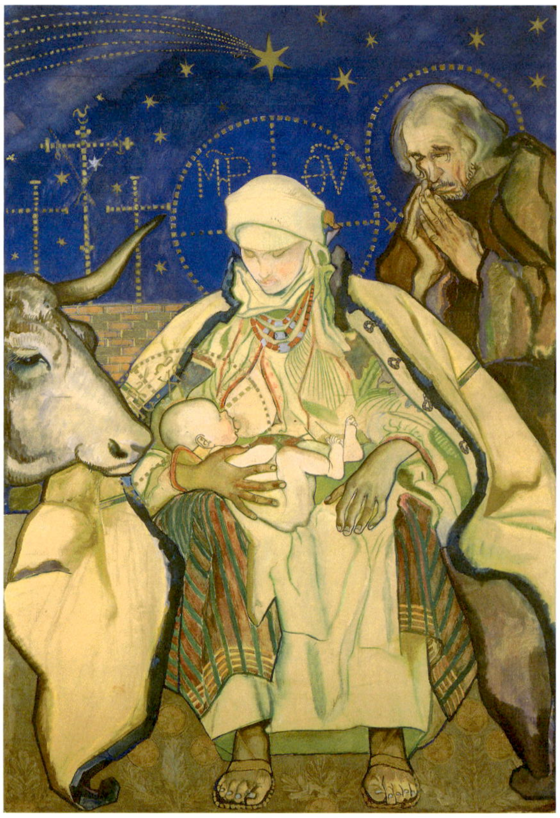

British Aesthetic Movement, and are also found in works by Mehoffer.

At the beginning of the twentieth century there was a serious revival of interest in the applied arts, stimulated by the influence of the British Arts and Crafts Movement and the progress of industrial design reforms in Britain and other industrialised countries across the Continent. In 1901 the Polish Applied Art Society (*Towarzystwo Polska Sztuka Stosowana*) was founded in Kraków by artists, architects and designers from all three partitions, the principal aim of which was the creation of a Polish national design style.

The society was modelled on the Arts and Crafts workshops, and under the leadership of Jerzy Warchałowski began to investigate vernacular architecture and folk art from the different cultures of the historic Polish–Lithuanian Commonwealth, which were still alive in the more provincial areas. Their periodical *Materyały* (1902–1905) from 1906 published

Fig.25 Kazimierz Sichulski
Angel
1911
Gouache, watercolour, gold, silver, paper on canvas
152 x 89
National Museum Poznań

Fig.26 Kazimierz Sichulski
Holy Family
1913
Central panel from a triptych
Distemper, pastel, paper on canvas
155.8 x 106
National Museum Warsaw

under the title *Sztuka stosowana* (*Applied Art*) – illustrated examples of such works included scholarly studies of folk art, and became the sourcebook for members of the society.

The output of the society's members was very diverse and included stained-glass windows, tapestries, metalwork, embroidery and woodwork, as well as children's toys and postcards. The society was also commissioned to design whole interiors, in the spirit of *Gesamtkunstwerk*, particularly those with national cultural significance, such as the Old Theatre in Kraków (1905–6), but also fashionable bohemian cafés such as Michalik's Den in Kraków (1910), famous as the birthplace of the Little Green Balloon cabaret.[20]

The most prominent member of the Polish Applied Art Society was Stanisław Wyspiański, who saw the applied arts as the transporters of beauty into the everyday, and hence capable of ennobling people's lives. He possessed exceptional talent and was acknowledged as a painter, draughtsman, designer, writer, stage designer, theatre director, and, for a brief moment, a member of Kraków's city council. In his works he commented on the Polish cult of history, but at the same time called for the reawakening of the national spirit, taking as his example the city of Kraków, where the monuments to the past seemed to him to be like the buried seeds of a future revival.

Wyspiański's imagination was fuelled by his admiration for classical and Gothic art, as well as contemporary Symbolist theories and an interest in the vernacular. He was a master of the pastel technique, which he employed in numerous portraits and Symbolist landscapes, as well as of visionary images of Polish national myths such as his *Polonia* 1893–4 (see fig.13). Among his most powerful monumental works was the decoration of the Franciscan Church in Kraków (1897–1904), for which he designed wall paintings and stained-glass windows, combining floral and abstract motifs with powerful representations of saints and of God creating the world (see fig.9). Another of Wyspiański's *Gesamtkunstwerk* was the decoration of the Medical Society building in Kraków (1904), which included the architectural interior and stained-glass windows. The central window was dedicated to Apollo, the ancient god of medicine, symbol of sun and patron of the arts (see fig.8). Wyspiański showed Apollo surrounded by figures representing planets in the solar system, thus making him the symbol of cosmic forces as a source of creativity. But for Wyspiański, Apollo was also an artist-poet, bound to the lyre, visible behind his shoulders, destined not only to produce art for art's sake but to perform a public role demanded of him by the political realities of his time. The idea of sacrifice and redemption through art was also illustrated by the parallels between the figure of Apollo and the traditional representation of a crucified Christ, whose body, with sinking head, hangs on the cross.

Towards the end of his life Wyspiański drew up designs for a major rebuilding of Wawel Hill in Kraków, which included the former Royal Castle and the Cathedral (1904–6), with the idea of turning it into a future Polish Acropolis. Wawel was to become the centre of cultural and political life of the nation with the newly planned seats of the Polish Parliament and the National Museum. This gesture summed up his hopes for the glorification of Poland's national heritage and emphasised the role Kraków played, which for Poles held the same significance as Athens did for the ancient Greeks.[21]

Other members of the Polish Applied Art Society produced remarkable work that demonstrates their attempt to create a national design style. Franciszek Bruzdowicz's decoration of a church interior in Cimkowicze, near Minsk in Belarus (1908, destroyed), based on local folk-art tradition, was praised for its expressionistic use of form and colour (fig.27). Among the masters of decorative wall painting was Jan Bukowski, designer of numerous church decorations, as well as of remarkable prints and graphic designs, inspired by folk-art motifs and the Art Nouveau style (fig.28). The most singular member of the society was Karol Tichy, whose designs were characterised by a visual refinement and a modernist predilection towards geometric simplicity (fig.29).

In 1913 another Arts and Crafts society known as the Kraków Workshops (*Warsztaty Krakowskie*) was founded in Kraków. In contrast to the Polish Applied Art Society, the new society was interested less in the decorative aspects of a national style than in the construction principles found in vernacular and folk art, in order to create a new understanding of design governed by simplicity and functionalism. Both societies were also associated with the protagonists of housing reform, looking for new models of Polish houses and urban designs inspired by the Garden City ideals being practised

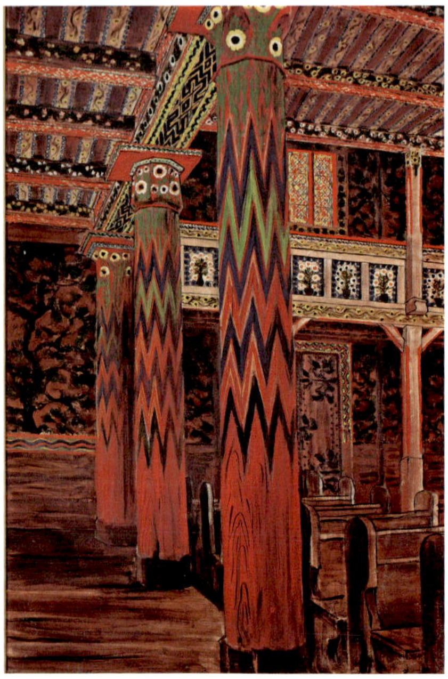

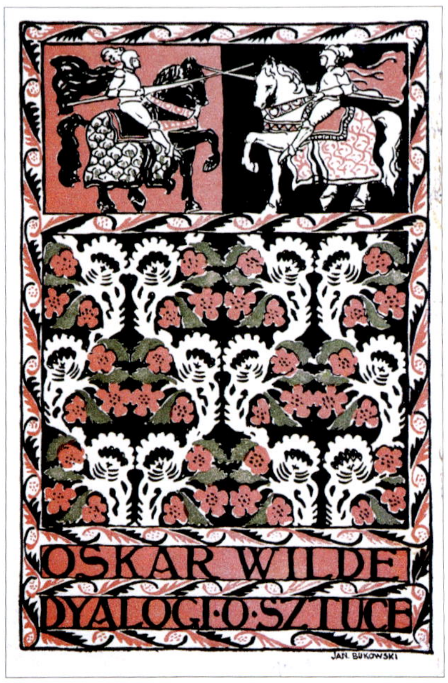

Fig.27 Franciszek Bruzdowicz
Interior of Cimkowicze Church
1908
Oil on canvas
103 x 69
National Museum Warsaw

Fig.28 Jan Bukowski
Book cover for Polish edition of
Dialogues on Art by Oscar Wilde
1906
Zincography, three-colour concave print on paper
19.2 x 11.9
Academy of Fine Arts Library, Kraków

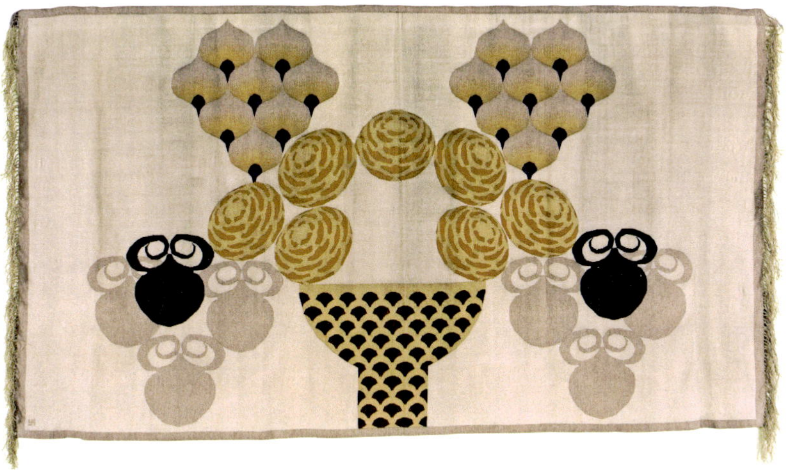

Fig.29 Karol Tichy
Kilim
c.1900
Flatwoven wool
180 x 319
National Museum Kraków

in Europe since the early twentieth century. The Garden City movement, which originated in Great Britain, aimed at the foundation of a new type of small-scale city composed of individual houses and limited areas of industry and agriculture, which could provide a new, efficient and healthy way of living for its residents, as opposed to the dehumanising metropolis created by 19th century industrial revolution.

The new style of domestic architecture, advocated by the Polish Applied Art Society, referenced the architecture of provincial manor houses in Poland. From 1903 this was known as the 'manor-house style' (*styl dworkowy*). Such houses were often designed in the context of Garden City colonies. Several such colonies were either planned or built in or alongside Polish cities before the outbreak of the First World War, including Kraków, Warsaw and Lvov. These developments were included in the architectural exhibition put on by the Polish Applied Art Society in Kraków in 1912 in order to promote the ideals of the Garden City. The exhibition was visited by Ebenezer Howard, the British pioneer of the Garden City movement, who enjoyed his visit to such an extent that as noted by the Kraków architectural journal *Architekt* he called Kraków, then a small-scale town with almost no industry and large green areas, a 'Garden City from natural development'.

The Young Poland movement has been intensely relevant to Polish culture ever since the early years of the twentieth century. Every subsequent generation has, at some point, confronted and reinterpreted the cultural achievements of this period, as if it left us with timeless visual codes, summarising crucial features of our national heritage. At the same time the general questions asked then, especially those regarding the sources of our modernity, have not lost currency. Most importantly, around 1900 Polish artists managed to universalise the various sources of their national culture, and elaborated a unique visual language that still conveys viable meanings today.

ARTIST BIOGRAPHIES

JULIA DUDKIEWICZ

FELIKS STANISŁAW JASIŃSKI (born 1862 Ząbkowo; died 1901 Puteaux, France) was a draughtsman and one of Europe's most distinguished printmakers. Following the unsuccessful Polish uprising of 1863, his family moved to Belgium, and from 1871 he settled in Kraków. Jasiński returned to Brussels between 1880 and 1881 to study painting at the M. Van Alphen School. In 1882 he went to Paris to study medal-making and soon took French citizenship. It was through his friendship with the printmaker Léon Gaucherel that Jasiński decided to train as a printmaker. In 1885 he was commissioned to produce a set of prints after the Old Masters. In recognition of his gold medal at the 1887 Salon, Jasiński was invited to become a regular contributor to the *Gazette des Beaux-Arts*, which subsequently published fourteen of his prints. With his second gold medal at the *Blanc et Noir* exhibition in Paris in 1889, Jasiński was confirmed in his standing as one of Europe's leading printmakers. He was commissioned by the London-based printer Arthur Tooth & Sons to produce a series of prints after six of Edward Burne-Jones' works (1894–1900), as well as Dante Gabriel Rossetti's *Paolo and Francesca* (1903). At the time of this collaboration he made several visits to London. He was awarded a gold medal at the 1900 Universal Exhibition in Paris for three works. Jasiński was colour-blind, which limited his own artistic activity to pencil drawings and pastel, reminiscent of Paul Gauguin and his close friend Félix Vallotton. His prints were exhibited throughout Europe, including France, Munich, Brussels and Poland.

JACEK MALCZEWSKI (born 1854 Radom; died Kraków 1929) was a pioneering painter of the Polish Symbolist movement, a co-founder of the *Sztuka* (Art) secessionist society (1897), and a member of the Vienna Secession. He was renowned for the patriotic-martyrologic content of his work, which combined a unique Symbolist imagery with striking realism. From 1873 he studied at the School of Fine Arts in Kraków, and from 1875 under Jan Matejko who looked upon Malczewski as his successor. Malczewski soon developed a stormy relationship with his master and in 1876 left for Paris, where he studied at the École des Beaux-Arts and the Académie Suisse. On his return to Kraków in 1877 he briefly resumed his studies under Matejko, and spent the next few years travelling around Europe, visiting Italy (1880, 1890), Turkey (1884), and Munich (1885–6, 1892, 1893). It was the artistic environment of Paris and Munich, as well as the poetry of Juliusz Słowacki, which fuelled Malczewski's interest in Symbolism, in his treatment of subjects such as Poland's independence and martyrdom as well as themes of death and the vocation of the artist. He also produced symbolic portraits, self-portraits and landscapes. Malczewski was a dedicated mentor for other artists, having been appointed a Deputy Professor at the School of Fine Arts in Kraków in 1898 (he resigned in 1900 due to a conflict with the rector). Despite his marriage to Maria (neé Gralewska) in 1887, around 1900 Malczewski fell in love with a married woman, Maria Balowa, who became his muse and featured in numerous allegorical paintings. After the outbreak of the First World War, Malczewski moved to Vienna with his family and finally came back to Kraków in 1916. His most notable works include *Melancholy* 1894 and *The Vicious Circle* 1895–7, both of which were awarded silver medals at the Paris Universal Exhibition of 1900.

JÓZEF MEHOFFER (born 1869 Ropczyce near Rzeszów; died 1946 Wadowice near Kraków) was a painter, printmaker, applied arts designer, a co-founder of *Sztuka* and a member of the Vienna Secession. He gained international recognition with his winning designs in a competition for a series of stained-glass windows for the Church of St Nicholas in Fribourg, Switzerland (1895–1935). From 1887 Mehoffer studied at the School of Fine Arts in Kraków. Here he met Jan Matejko, who invited him and Stanisław Wyspiański to assist him in the realisation of his polychromy designs at the Mariacki Church in Kraków (1889). Mehoffer also studied at the Kunstakademie in Vienna (1889–90), as well as at a number of schools in Paris (1891–6), where he shared a studio with his friend Wyspiański. Mehoffer's training there included the Académie Colarossi, the École Nationale des Arts Décoratifs and the École Nationale des Beaux-Arts. From 1900 he was a lecturer at the Academy of Fine Arts in Kraków, before becoming a Professor and then its Rector. His major works in Kraków include the decorative scheme designs for parts of Wawel Cathedral (1904–24) and polychromy for the Treasury (1900–1903), as well as a decorative scheme for the Chamber of Industry and Commerce (1906). As a painter, he won a gold medal at the Paris Universal Exhibition of 1900 for the portrait *Singer* as well as a number of gold medals for his most famous Symbolist work, *Strange Garden*, at the Universal Exhibitions in Chicago (1904), St Louis (1904) and Munich (1905). His versatile design work ranged from illustrations, vignettes and typography for books and magazines including *Chimera* and *Życie*, to posters and stage design. Following the outbreak of the Second World War, Mehoffer was sent to a concentration camp, but was subsequently freed after the Vatican requested his release as a renowned artist of religious subjects.

JÓZEF PANKIEWICZ (born 1866 Lublin; died 1940 Marseille, France) was a painter and printmaker and one of the first Polish Impressionists and Symbolists. He was a member of *Sztuka* and a founder of the Polish twentieth-century Colourist Movement aimed at conveying mood through subtle use of colour, particularly in artists' impressions of nature. He trained at the Drawing School in Warsaw (1884–5) before travelling to St Petersburg to study at the School of Fine Arts (1885–6), and then Paris in 1889. His early work was largely realistic, including documentary illustrations of Warsaw street life for *Tygodnik Ilustrowany* (*Illustrated Weekly*), then later gave way to his novel Impressionist technique of painting. Following his return to Warsaw in 1890, Pankiewicz developed an interest in depicting atmospheric night scenes showing the influence of Japanese art and French Symbolist literature as seen in the works *Old Town Square at Night* 1892 and *Nocturne: Swans in the Saxon Garden in Warsaw by Night* 1894. His preoccupation with monochromatic colour schemes in landscape and portraiture demonstrate an appreciation of the art of James Abbott McNeill Whistler. Pankiewicz was well-travelled in Europe, visiting countries including England, Italy, France, Germany, Belgium and Holland between 1897 and 1903, and he received a number of international awards including silver and gold medals at the Paris Universal Exhibitions in 1889, 1899 and 1900. He also exhibited at the Salons des Indépendants, the Autumn Salon and the Galerie Georges Petit. In 1906 he undertook a teaching post as a Professor at the Acdemy of Fine Arts in Kraków. He lived in Spain during the First World War, and eventually assumed the management of the Kraków Academy's Paris branch (1925–37). In recognition of his artistic achievements he was awarded the title of Cavalier of the Legion of Honour by the French government.

KAZIMIERZ SICHULSKI (born 1879 Lvov; died 1942 Lvov) was a painter, caricaturist, designer of stained glass and mosaics, illustrator, the artistic director of *Liberum Veto* magazine and a member of the Austrian arts association Hagenbund. He was a member of *Sztuka* and co-founder of the Little Green Balloon (*Zielony Balonik*) cabaret, staged at the bohemian Michalik's Den café in Kraków (1905–12). He studied at the Academy of Fine Arts in Kraków (1900–8) under Mehoffer and Wyspiański, and soon became the latter's protégé and follower. He also attended the Kunstgewerbeschule des Österreichischen Museums für Kunst und Industrie art school in Vienna (1902) and the Académie Colarossi in Paris. Sichulski's diverse artistic output included idealised landscapes and genre paintings of Huzul peasant life, which often conveyed deeper Symbolist and religious meanings. It was his intention to create an artist's colony in the Carpathian Mountains. He won international renown for his satirical illustrations and caricatures of Polish cultural figures and politicians, which led to international commissions for caricatures of MPs from both London (1911, not realised) and Vienna (1912, published as a best-selling album of prints). As a caricaturist, Sichulski also contributed to the decorative scheme at Michalik's Den with a group caricature of all the cultural figures associated with the cabaret. In the wake of Poland's independence in 1918, Sichulski directed his efforts to a search for a national style.

KAZIMIERZ STABROWSKI (born 1869, Kruplany near Nowogródek; died 1929 Garwolin) was a painter, a member of *Sztuka* and a founder and first Director of the School of Fine Arts in Warsaw (1904–9). He trained at the School of Fine Arts in St Petersburg (1887–97) and at the Académie Julian in Paris (1897–8), moving to Warsaw in 1900. He produced history paintings and portraits, some of which were informed by his interest in mysticism and the occult, as well as atmospheric landscapes. Many of his stylised portraits were inspired by the 'Young Art' fancy-dress carnival ball of 1908 at the spectacular building of the National Philharmonic in Warsaw, attended by his art students who wore extravagant costumes made from tissue paper. The Young Art ball was a manifestation of the Polish national spirit, with the fancy dress bearing hidden meanings. Although Stabrowski's output remains largely untraced and dispersed, it is these decorative, Art Nouveau-inspired stylised portraits with a psychological dimension that remain his best-known works, including *Portrait of Painter Bronisław Brykner in Fancy Dress Costume* 1908 and *Against the Backdrop of a Stained Glass Window (Peacock)* 1908.

WITOLD WOJTKIEWICZ (born 1879 Warsaw; died 1909 Warsaw) was an innovative modernist painter and draughtsman, who was a Polish proto-expressionist. His father Stanisław, a senior bank clerk, disapproved of his son's artistic aspirations, while his mother Aniela was busy bringing up his ten siblings. Wojtkiewicz studied at the School of Fine Arts in St Petersburg, the Drawing School in Warsaw (1898) and the Academy of Fine Arts in Kraków (1903–6). He initially established himself as an illustrator and caricaturist, and contributed watercolours and drawings to the decorative scheme at the café Michalik's Den in Kraków. He was part of 'Norwid's Group' of artists, also known as the 'Group of Five', with whom he exhibited from 1905, including the successful show at the Galerie Schulte in Berlin (1907), where he was noticed by André Gide and offered a solo exhibition at the Galerie Druet in Paris. Between 1905 and 1907, Wojtkiewicz produced his most famous works, the *Monomania* and *Circus* series, and later the *Ceremony* cycle 1908. His imagery draws on distortion and caricature, combining the tragic with the grotesque, in mysterious group compositions featuring the vulnerable and the weak in the form of children, puppets and old people. Wojtkiewicz died prematurely aged twenty-nine, due to a genetic heart condition.

STANISŁAW WYSPIAŃSKI (born 1869 Kraków; died 1907 Kraków) was one of the most versatile artists of his generation, renowned as a painter, draughtsman, printmaker, furniture and interior designer, stage-set and costume designer, theatre director and playwright, stained-glass designer, poet, magazine editor, a co-founder of *Sztuka* and a member of the Vienna Secession. From 1887 he studied philosophy and art history at the Jagiellonian University and drawing at the School of Fine Arts in Kraków under Jan Matejko, a family friend who invited the young student and Mehoffer to assist him in the decoration of the Mariacki Church in the city (1889). Wyspiański spent extensive periods in Paris between 1891 and 1894, where he met Paul Gauguin and the Nabis, and studied at the Académie Colarossi. Wyspiański contracted syphilis in Paris, which was to result in his premature death aged thirty-eight. The disease considerably limited his later creative activity, and towards the end of his life a crayon had to be tied to his fingers to enable him to draw.

Wyspiański's most famous decorative scheme was the stylised floral polychromy (reminiscent of William Morris' work) and the stained-glass windows he produced for the Franciscan Church in Kraków (1897–1904), and the interior and stained glass of the Medical Society 1905. His other decorative designs were usually too pioneering and innovative to be passed by the commissioning committees of his day, and only survive as unrealised cartoons. These include the designs for stained-glass windows for Wawel Cathedral in Kraków evoking Poland's past kings as regal skeletons; *The Vows of Jan Kazimierz* 1893–4, a rejected stained-glass design for Lvov Cathedral; and his iconic *Polonia* 1893–4. Due to an allergy to oil paint, most of Wyspiański's painted compositions were executed in pastel, on subjects that included peasant life, maternity, childhood and national independence. Unusually for the time, Wyspiański married a peasant woman, Teodora Teofila Pytko in 1900; they had two children. Like Morris, Wyspiański championed the artistic book revival in Poland and served as the artistic director of *Życie* magazine. He was also actively involved in the restoration of historic sites, including plans for the Wawel Castle. His best-known play, *Wesele* (The Wedding, 1901), about a peasant wedding, was a comment on Poland's political and cultural situation. In 1902 Wyspiański became a Professor of Decorative and Religious Painting at the Academy of Fine Arts in Kraków, and in 1905 he was appointed a city councillor.

LIST OF EXHIBITED WORKS

Lawrence Alma-Tadema
Portrait of Ignacy Jan Paderewski 1891
Oil on canvas
45.5 x 59
National Museum Warsaw
(p.9)

Edward Burne-Jones
Portrait of Ignacy Jan Paderewski 1892
Pencil on paper
34.7 x 31
National Museum Warsaw
(p.8)

Walter Crane
The Triumph of Labour 1897
Zincograph on paper
9 x 14
The Sosenko Family Archives and Collections
(p.17)

Sir Alfred Gilbert
Ignacy Jan Paderewski 1891
Bronze sculpture
60 x 31.9 x 19.3
Tate
(p.8)

Feliks Jasiński
The Golden Stairs 1894
Engraving on parchment
75 x 36.5
National Museum Warsaw
(p.10)

Feliks Jasiński
Paolo and Francesca 1903
Etching in sepia tone on paper
46.8 x 37.9
National Museum Warsaw
(p.11)

Jacek Malczewski
The Death of Ellenai 1907
Oil on canvas
208 x 114
Property of the Raczyński Foundation
at the National Museum Poznań
(p.24)

Jacek Malczewski
Eloe with Ellenai 1908–1909
Oil on canvas
218 x 129
National Museum Poznań
(p.25)

Józef Mehoffer
Strange Garden 1902–1903
Oil on canvas
217 x 208
National Museum Warsaw
(p.27)

Józef Pankiewicz
Nocturne – Swans in the Saxon Garden in Warsaw at Night 1894
Oil on canvas
86 x 151
National Museum Warsaw
(p.16)

Kazimierz Sichulski
Angel 1911
Gouache, watercolour, gold, silver, paper on canvas
152 x 89
National Museum Poznań
(p.30)

Kazimierz Stabrowski
Portrait of the Artist's wife, c.1907
Oil on canvas
160 x 98
National Museum Warsaw
(p.28)

Witold Wojtkiewicz
Christ and the Children 1908
Oil on canvas
65 x 70
National Museum Warsaw
(p.29)

Witold Wojtkiewicz
Meditations 1908
Oil on canvas
80 x 90
National Museum Kraków
(p.29)

Stanisław Wyspiański
Apollo 1904
Pastel on paper
343 x 146
National Museum Kraków
(p.14)

NOTES

British Symbolism and Polish Modernism c.1900

ALISON SMITH

1 Piotr Kopszak and Andrzej Szczerski, *Śladami prerafaelitów: Artyści polscy i sztuka brytyjska na przełomie XIX i XX w.* (*In the Footsteps of the Pre-Raphaelites*), exh. cat., Muzeum Pałac w Wilanowie, Warsaw, 2006. The lack of interest in Polish art in Britain during the nineteenth century was largely the result of the conquest and final partition of Poland in 1795 by Russia, Prussia and Austria, which effectively obliterated Poland from the map of Europe, threatening the identity of the region's artists as Poles (see the essay 'The Young Poland Movement: Art, Nation, Modernity' in this publication). During the twentieth century access to Polish art was restricted due to the Second World War and the Iron Curtain, although there were exceptions, the most important being the large presentation of Polish art at the Royal Academy in 1970 (*1000 Years of Art in Poland*, 3 Jan.–1 March) and the exhibition of the work of Malczewski at the Barbican Art Gallery in 1990 (*Malczewski: A Vision of Poland*, 10 May–8 July). The most substantial exhibition of British art in Poland was a selection of works by modern British artists from the Tate Gallery shown at the National Museum in Warsaw in 1946 (18 Nov.–9 Dec.; see Krzysztof Cieszkowski, 'The Tate Gallery and Poland', in *Archiwum Emigracji*, 1 (9), Toruń 2007, pp.197–8). There has been no subsequent exhibition of British works from the Tate in Poland, and neither has there ever been an exhibition of Polish art at the Tate.

2 Andrzej Szczerski, *Wzorce tożsamości*, Kraków 2002, pp.389–91.

3 Jan Cavanaugh, *Out Looking In: Early Modern Polish Art, 1890–1918*, Berkeley, Los Angeles and London 2000, p.68.

4 Ignacy Jan Paderewski and Mary Lawton, *The Paderewski Memoirs*, London 1939, p.177.

5 Georgiana Burne-Jones, *Memorials of Edward Burne-Jones*, 2 vols, London 1904, vol.2, p.207; Paderewski and Lawton 1939, p.176. See also the entry on this drawing by Andrzej Dzięciołowski in Kopszak and Szczerski 2006, pp.32–4.

6 T. Martin Wood (introduction), *Drawings of Sir Edward Burne-Jones*, London 1907, p.6.

7 Paderewski and Lawton 1939, p.178. Princess Louise's portrait is now in the National Gallery in Warsaw. Alma-Tadema's daughter Laurence became a vociferous supporter of Polish independence.

8 Léopold Wellisz, *Félix-Stanislas Jasiński, graveur: sa vie et son oeuvre*, Paris 1934, p.26; the translated quote is taken from Christopher Newall, 'Burne-Jones and his printmakers', in Julian Hartnoll, *The Reproductive Engravings after Sir Edward Coley Burne-Jones*, London 1988, p.13. See also the entries on Jasiński's prints after Burne-Jones by Ewa Milicer in Kopszak and Szczerski 2006, pp.35–50.

9 Amelia Sarah Levetus, 'Notes on Some Polish Artists of Today' (signed A.S.L), *The Studio*, 41, no.172, 1907, pp.115–26. See also Levetus' review of the 23rd exhibition of the Vienna Secession, *The Studio*, vol.35, 1905, pp.57–60.

10 Privately printed by the Favil Press, London 1938. The poem was probably conceived during Mansfield's residence in New Zealand at the time of Wyspiański's death.

11 Paderewski and Lawton 1939, p.174.

12 Morris' *The Lesser Arts* was published in Kraków 1902, *The Hopes and Concerns of Art* in Warsaw 1902, and a selection of his writings *The Foundations of Aesthetic Culture* in Lvov 1906. As regards Ruskin, the translated texts were mostly minor ones, excluding, for example, *Modern Painters*. However, as Piotr Juszkiewicz suggests, the broad dissemination of the writer's ideas contributed to a strand of unnamed Ruskinism in Polish culture (Juszkiewicz, 'Identity and Reception: Polish Research on Victorian Art and Art Theory', *Journal of Victorian Culture*, autumn 2007, p.315, citing Bożena Wojnowska's 'Ruskinizm w Młodej Polsce', *Studia Estetyczne*, vol.XIII, 1976, pp.259–81). For Pater see Juszkiewicz 2007, p.315.

13 *Chimera*, vol.3, issue 9, Sept. 1901. Beardsley's *How Queen Quenevere made her a nun* was reproduced in the May–June 1904 issue.

14 *Życie*, 10 Sept. 1898. This edition also included a reproduction of *The Annunciation* (1876–9, Lady Lever Art Gallery, Liverpool). Heliogravure and platinotype prints after the Paderewski portrait were shown together with other reproductions of Burne-Jones' work at the Zachęta Gallery, Warsaw, in 1905.

15 Jasieński probably knew *Vespertina Quies* through Emile Boilvin's engraving of the painting, published by Tooth in 1897. He might also have seen it exhibited at the New Gallery in 1894. Feliks Jasieński, *Manggha: promenades à travers le monde, l'art et les idées*, Warsaw 1901, pp.167–8; 161–2. See also the discussion of this article in Piotr Kopszak's essay 'Being on the side of the degenerate', in Kopszak and Szczerski 2006, pp.3–4.

16 Robert de la Sizeranne, trans. Helena d'Abancourt, *Malarstwo współczesne Anglii* (*Contemporary Painting in England*), Kraków 1901, Preface, p.4; Jasieński 1901, p.163, translation by Julia Dudkiewicz.

17 Matuszewski, *Słowacki i nowa sztuka*, Kraków 1902, p.231; see also Andrzej Szczerski's essay 'Like from a Painting by Burne-Jones: Interpretations of the Pre-Raphaelites in Polish Art around 1900', in Kopszak and Szczerski 2006, p.7.

18 Stanisław Wyspiański, *The Wedding* 1901, trans. Gerard T. Kapolka, Ann Arbor, Ardis, 1990; Szczerski, in Kopszak and Szczerski 2006, p.7. A *chochoł* is a straw man. Wyspiański's essay *The Tragic History of Hamlet* was published in 1905, and in 1903 Malczewski used the character to explore the experience of living under occupation in his painting *The Polish Hamlet – Portrait of Aleksander Wielopolski* (National Museum Warsaw).

19 Fourteen oils by Whistler and twenty-seven works on paper were exhibited in Munich in 1888. Whistler also exhibited in Hamburg and Berlin in the mid 1890s, and Vienna in 1895. See Szczerski 2002, p.59; Cavanaugh 2000, p.42.

20 Szczerski, in Kopszak and Szczerski 2006, p.8.

21 Leon Winiarski, *Życiorysy znakomitych ludzi; William Morris*, Warsaw 1900, pp.44, 48–9.

The Young Poland Movement: Art, Nation, Modernity

PIOTR KOPSZAK AND ANDRZEJ SZCZERSKI

1 For recent English-language literature on the Young Poland Movement, see Jan Cavanaugh, *Out Looking In: Early Modern Polish Art 1890–1918*, Berkeley, Los Angeles and London 2000; and Elisabeth Clegg, *Art, Design and Architecture in Central Europe 1890–1920*, New Haven and London 2006.

2 Julian Klaczko (Jehuda Lejb), *Sztuka Polska*, 'Wiadomości Polskie', Paris 1857, reprinted in Irena Jakimowicz, *Spór o rację bytu sztuki narodowej. Z dziejów polskiej krytyki i teorii sztuki*, vol.2, Warsaw 1961, pp.39–68, 165–71.

3 See Piotr Krakowski and Jacek Purchla (eds.), *Wokół Matejki*, Kraków 1994 for a recent discussion of Matejko's painting in a Central European context.

4 For a detailed account of Polish artistic life around 1900, see Aleksander Wojciechowski, *Polskie życie artystyczne w latach 1890–1914*, Wrocław 1967.

5 Andrzej Walicki, *Philosophy and Romantic Nationalism:*

The Case of Poland, Oxford 1982.

6 David Crowley, *National Style and Nation-State: Design in Poland from the Vernacular Revival to the International Style*, Manchester and New York 1992, pp.15–27; Zbigniew Moździerz, *Dom 'Pod Jedlami' Pawlikowskich*, Wydawnictwa Muzeum Tatrzańskiego im. dra Tytusa Chałubińskiego w Zakopanem Nr 24, Zakopane 2003, pp.37–8, 225, 245.

7 Jeremy Howard, 'National Movements and International Vocabularies in Galician turn-of-the-century Architecture: the City of Lemberg', in *Genius Loci*, ed. C. Popescu, Bucharest 2002, pp.82–9.

8 See Andrzej Szczerski, *Wzorce tożsamości. Recepcja sztuki brytyjskiej w Europie Środkowej około roku 1900*, Kraków 2002, pp.76–119.

9 Agnieszka Morawińska, *L'Avant-printemps: Pologne 1880–1920*, exh. cat., Palais de Beaux-Arts Bruxelles, Brussels 2001, pp.22–31; *Fin de Siècle: Polish Art 1890–1914*, ed. Elżbieta Charazińska and Łukasz Kossowski, National Museum Warsaw 1996.

10 See Dorota Suchocka, *Witold Pruszkowski*, exh. cat., Muzeum Narodowe w Poznaniu, Poznań 1992.

11 Elżbieta Charazińska, *Adam Chmielowski – św. Brat Albert 1845–1916*, Muzeum Archidiecezji Krakowskiej, Kraków 1995.

12 Agnieszka Ławniczakowa, *Jacek Malczewski*, Warsaw 1976; Dorota Kudelska, *Dukt pisma i pędzla. Biografia intelektualna Jacka Malczewskiego*, Lublin 2008. Malczewski's contemporaries noticed the discerning attitude of the painter towards the prevailing glorification of exiles – 'tearing down the aura of the exiles'. They noticed that in his Siberian pictures he depicts both heroes and criminals (Kudelska 2008, pp.740–4).

13 Ławniczakowa 1976, p.13.

14 Tadeusz Adamowicz, *Witraże fryburskie Józefa Mehoffera. Monografia zespołu*, Wrocław, Warsaw and Kraków 1982; *Józef Mehoffer: Opus Magnum*, exh. cat., Muzeum Narodowe w Krakowie, Kraków 2000.

15 Beiersdorf Purchla, 1988.

16 Maria Rostworowska, *Portret za mgłą. Opowieść o Oldze Boznańskiej*, Warsaw 2003; Anna Król, *Olga Boznańska*, exh. cat., Szczecin 2006; Piotr Kopszak, *Olga Boznańska*, Warsaw 2007.

17 Elżbieta Charazińska (ed.), *Józef Pankiewicz 1866–1940. Życie i dzieło. Artyście w 140. rocznicę urodzin*, exh. cat., Muzeum Narodowe Warszawie, Warsaw 2006.

18 Wiesław Juszczak, *Młody Weiss*, Warsaw 1979, *Totenmesse. Munch – Weiss – Przybyszewski*, ed. Ł. Kossowski, J. Chromy (Polish text) and E. Clegg (English text), exh. cat., Muzeum Literatury im. A. Mickiewicza, Warsaw 1995; for the later Impressionist phase of Weiss' work, see Zofia Weiss-Nowina Konopka, *Piękno do mnie przyszło ... Wojciech Weiss – malarstwo białego okresu*, exh. cat., Muzeum Pałac w Wilanowie, Warsaw 2007.

19 Witold Wojtkiewicz 2004; Ficowski 1993; Ficowski 1996.

20 Irena Huml, *Polska sztuka stosowana XX wieku*, Warsaw 1978, pp.9–64; on the Arts and Crafts Movement in Poland and the rest of Central Europe, see *Centropa*, New York, vol.4, no.3, Sept. 2004.

21 Recent account on Wyspiański in Wojciech Bałus, pp.71–221. See also exhibition catalogues Wyspiański 2000 and Charazińska 2007.

BIBLIOGRAPHY

Tadeusz Adamowicz, *Witraże fryburskie Józefa Mehoffera. Monografia zespołu*, Wrocław, Warsaw and Kraków 1982

Wojciech Bałus, *Sztuka sakralna Krakowa w wieku XIX cz. II Matejko i Wyspiański*, Kraków 2007

Anna Baran (ed.), *Stulecie Towarzystwa Artystów Polskich 'Sztuka'*, Kraków 2001

Zbigniew Beiersdorf and Jacek Purchla, *Dom pod Globusem, dawna siedziba krakowskiej Izby Handlowej i Przemysłowej*. Kraków 1988

Jurij Biriulow, *Secesja we Lwowie*, Warsaw 1996

Anna Brzyski, " 'Unsere Polen': Polish Artists and the Vienna Secession," in Michelle Facos and Sharon Hirsh ed., *Art and National Identity at the Turn of the Century*, Cambridge 2003

Georgiana Burne-Jones, *Memorials of Edward Burne-Jones*, 2 vols., London 1904

Jan Cavanaugh, *Out Looking In: Early Modern Polish Art* 1890–1918, Berkeley, Los Angeles and London 2000

Centropa, New York, vol.4, no.3, Sept. 2004

Elżbieta Charazińska, *Adam Chmielowski – św. Brat Albert 1845–1916*, Muzeum Archidiecezji Krakowskiej, Kraków 1995

Elżbieta Charazińska (ed.), *Józef Pankiewicz 1866–1940. Życie i dzieło. Artyście w 140. rocznicę urodzin*, exh. cat., Muzeum Narodowe w Warszawie, Warsaw *2006*

Elżbieta Charazińska (ed.), *'Jak meteor...' : Stanisław Wyspiański (1869–1907) : artyście w setną rocznicę śmierci : katalog wystawy dzieł ze zbiorów Muzeum Narodowego w Warszawie.* Warsaw 2007

Elżbieta Charazińska and Łukasz Kossowski ed., *Fin de Siècle: Polish Art 1890–1914*, National Museum Warsaw 1996

Krzysztof Cieszkowski, 'The Tate Gallery and Poland', in *Archiwum Emigracji*, 1 (9), Toruń 2007, pp.196–202

Elisabeth Clegg, *Art, Design and Architecture in Central Europe 1890–1920*, New Haven and London 2006

David Crowley, *National Style and Nation-State: Design in Poland from the Vernacular Revival to the International Style*, Manchester and New York 1992

Krystyna Czerni, *Witraż 'Apollo' Stanisława Wyspiańskiego dla Domu Lekarskiego w Krakowie, 'Folia Historiae Artium'* 1993, vol. XXIX, p. 129–49

Dictionary of Polish Artists (*Słownik Artystów Polskich*), Warsaw 1979

Dictionary of Polish Artists (*Słownik Artystów Polskich*), Warsaw 1993

Dictionary of Polish Artists (*Słownik Artystów Polskich*), Warsaw 1998

Tadeusz Dobrowolski, *Sztuka Młodej Polski*, Warsaw 1963

Jerzy Ficowski, *W sierocińcu świata. Rzecz o Witoldzie Wojtkiewiczu*, Warsaw 1993

Jerzy Ficowski, *Witold Wojtkiewicz*, Łowicz 1996

Tomasz Gryglewicz, *Groteska w sztuce polskiej XX wieku*, Kraków Wrocław 1984

Julian Hartnoll, *The Reproductive Engravings after Sir Edward Coley Burne-Jones*, London 1988

Ewa Houszka, *Kazimierz Sichulski*, exh. cat., National Museum in Wrocław, Wrocław 1994

Jeremy Howard, 'National Movements and International Vocabularies in Galician turn-of-the-century Architecture: the City of Lemberg', in *Genius Loci*, ed. C. Popescu, Bucharest 2002

Irena Huml, *Polska sztuka stosowana XX wieku*, Warsaw 1978

Feliks Jasieński, *Manggha: promenades à travers le monde, l'art et les idées*, Warsaw 1901

Wiesław Juszczak, *Młody Weiss*, Warsaw 1979

Piotr Juszkiewicz, 'Identity and Reception: Polish Research on Victorian Art and Art Theory', *Journal of Victorian Culture*, autumn 2007, pp.314–19

Julian Klaczko (Jehuda Lejb), *Sztuka Polska* (*Polish Art*), 'Wiadomości Polskie' (Paris), 1857, reprinted in Irena Jakimowicz, *Spór o rację bytu sztuki narodowej. Z dziejów polskiej krytyki i teorii sztuki*, vol.2, Warsaw 1961, pp.39–68, 165–71

Piotr Kopszak and Andrzej Szczerski, *Śladami prerafaelitów: Artyści polscy i sztuka brytyjska na przełomie XIX i XX w.*, exh. cat., Muzeum Pałac w Wilanowie, Warsaw 2006

Piotr Kopszak, *Olga Boznańska*, Warsaw 2007

Ł. Kossowski ed., *Totenmesse. Munch – Weiss – Przybyszewski*, J. Chromy (Polish text) and E. Clegg (English text), exh. cat., Muzeum Literatury im. A. Mickiewicza, Warsaw 1995

Piotr Krakowski, and Jacek Purchla (eds.), *Wokół Matejki* , Kraków 1994

Anna Król, *Olga Boznańska*, exh. cat., Szczecin 2006

Stefania Krzysztofowicz-Kozakowska, *Polish Art Nouveau*, Kraków 1999

Dorota Kudelska, *Dukt pisma i pędzla. Biografia intelektualna Jacka Malczewskiego*, Lublin 2008

Laima Laučkaitė ed., *XX amžiaus pradžios Vilnius: modernėjančios kultūros židinys Wilno początku XX wieku: ognisko modernizującej się kultury*, Vilnius 2004

Agnieszka Ławniczakowa, *Jacek Malczewski*, Warsaw 1976

Amelia Sarah Levetus, 'Notes on Some Polish Artists of Today' (signed A.S.L), *The Studio*, 41, no.172, 1907, pp.115–26

Józef Mehoffer: Opus Magnum, exh. cat., Muzeum Narodowe w Krakowie, Kraków 2000

Agnieszka Morawińska, 'Hortus deliciarum Józefa Mehoffera', in *Ars Auro Prior. Studia Ioanni Białostocki sexagenario dicata*, Warsaw 1981, pp.713–18

Agnieszka Morawińska, *L'Avant-printemps: Pologne 1880–1920*, exh. cat., Palais de Beaux-Arts Bruxelles, Brussels 2001

Agnieszka Morawińska ed., *Symbolism in Polish Painting 1890–1914*, The Detroit Institute of Arts 1984

Zbigniew Moździerz, *Dom 'Pod Jedlami' Pawlikowskich, Wydawnictwa Muzeum Tatrzańskiego im. dra Tytusa Chałubińskiego w Zakopanem Nr 24*, Zakopane 2003

Ignacy Jan Paderewski and Mary Lawton, *The Paderewski Memoirs*, London 1939

Antoni Potocki, *Witold Wojtkiewicz. Zarys twórczości*, Museion, 1911, IV, pp.80–96

H. von Roda, *Die Glasmalereien von Józef Mehoffer in der Kathedrale St Nikolaus in Freiburg i. Ue*, Gesellschaft für Schweizerische, Kunstgeschichte, Bern 1995

Maria Rostworowska, *Portret za mgłą. Opowieść o Oldze Boznańskiej*, Warsaw 2003

Robert de la Sizeranne, trans. Helena d'Abancourt, *Malarstwo współczesne Anglii* (*Contemporary Painting in England*), Kraków 1901

Teresa Stepnowska, *Witold Wojtkiewicz*, Warsaw 1976

Kazimierz Stabrowski. Sylwetka malarza – poety, Poznań 1927

Dorota Suchocka, *Witold Pruszkowski*, exh. cat., Muzeum Narodowe w Poznaniu, Poznań 1992

Andrzej Szczerski, *Wzorce tożsamości. Recepcja sztuki brytyjskiej w Europie Środkowej około roku 1900*, Kraków 2002

Andrzej Szczerski, 'Sources of Modernity: The Interpretations of Vernacular Crafts in Polish Design around 1900' in *The Journal of Modern Craft*, vol.1, issue1, March 2008, pp.55–75

Andrzej Walicki, *Philosophy and Romantic Nationalism: The Case of Poland*, Oxford 1982

Zofia Weiss-Nowina Konopka, *Piękno do mnie przyszło . . . Wojciech Weiss – malarstwo białego okresu*, exh. cat., Muzeum Pałac w Wilanowie, Warsaw 2007

Léopold Wellisz, *Félix-Stanislas Jasiński, graveur: sa vie et son oeuvre*, Paris 1934

Leon Winiarski, *Życiorysy znakomitych ludzi; William Morris*, Warsaw 1900

Aleksander Wojciechowski, *Polskie życie artystyczne w latach 1890–1924*, Wrocław 1967

Witold Wojtkiewicz, *Une fable polonaise*, exh. cat., Grenoble 2004

T. Martin Wood (introduction), *Drawings of Sir Edward Burne-Jones*, London 1907

Stanisław Wyspiański: Opus Magnum, exh. cat., Kraków 2000

ACKNOWLEDGEMENTS

Elżbieta Charazińska
Krzysztof Cieszkowski
David Crowley
Andrzej Dzięciołowski
Maria Gołąb
Zofia Gołubiew
Tomasz Gryglewicz
Tomasz Igrzycki
Olga Jaros
Paweł Jaskanis
Teresa Kuleszir
Anna Rudzińska
Wojciech Suchocki
Marek Świca
Andrew Visnevski

CREDITS

Bridgeman Art Library fig.7
Courtesy of Kluszczyński Publishing House, Kraków fig.9
Photograph by Piotr Ligier fig.10, fig.12, fig.22, fig.23
Photograph by Dawid Moździerz fig.14

The Sosenko Family Archives and Collections, Zbiory Rodziny Sosenko fig.11, fig.21
Tate 2008 fig.2, fig.6
Photograph from the National Museum Warsaw Archive fig.18
Photograph by Krzysztof Wilczyński/ Studio Ligier fig.1, fig.4, fig.5, fig.20, fig.27
Photograph by Teresa Żółtowska-Huszcza fig.3, fig.15, fig.19, fig.26